D0325436

MIKE BLINDER knows media advertising sales like no other. A well-known radio and television talent in Maine, he moved out from behind the microphone and camera to excel in media sales. Mike was quick to realize the importance of the newly emerging internet phenomenon, and soon launched the Internet Sales Division of a leading media group.

His career has grown exponentially since then, and Mike is now in high demand as a sales consultant for some of the world's most respected media companies and corporations. His unique approach to sales has been has been adopted by 50 thousand businesses worldwide, and the Blinder Group, Mike's company, has helped them bring their products – both traditional and Web-based – to countless clients, established and new. In the past decade alone, Mike and his team have provided "on-the-street training" to thousands of media reps, producing millions of dollars in sales.

Mike's "tried and true" sales methods continue to provide winning results, even with rapid changes in technologies, and even in the most difficult economic conditions in living memory. In this book he gives back to the sales community by sharing over two decades of experience and expertise in the "oldest noble profession."

SURVIVAL SELLING

EVEN IN THE TOUGHEST TIMES

Business 2 Business Sales
Using Back 2 Basic Skills

MIKE BLINDER

Copyright © 2008 by The Blinder Group. All rights reserved. Written permission must be secured from the publisher to use or reproduce any part of this book in any form, except for brief quotations in critical reviews or articles.

Edited by Danny Wool
Designed by Patrick Costello

ISBN: 978-0-615-26469-1

To three women:

Barbara Blinder, my mother, whose constant encouragement
has made me realize that my future lies in my hands;

Robin Blinder, my wife, whose unwavering faith and support
helps me reach new goals each day;

Haven Blinder, my daughter, whose very presence in my life
makes me strive to be a better person each and every day.

~ CONTENTS ~

Calling All Survivors!

It is not the strongest of the species that survives, nor the most intelligent that survives. It is the one that is the most adaptable to change.

—Charles Darwin

Boy, was I scared! I had just turned down a job as program director for MetroMedia radio in Washington, DC. I decided to follow my mentor's advice and stay at my small Maine-based radio station group, but even then my world would never be the same. Instead of facing the microphones and cameras of the entertainment side of the media industry, I was about to "hit the street" (as he called it) to learn the sales side of the business – under his tutelage, of course. Despite my stubbornness, he managed to convince me that the greatest hindrance to my professional growth was my lack of understanding of sales. Already thirty, I considered myself lucky that until then I'd successfully avoided the fast-talking, overbearing sales people at the various radio stations I had worked with since college. I thought I was above all that, and completely avoided that part of the business. But now that I was back from DC with a solid offer in hand, my boss – my mentor – sold me on staying with the promise that I could really grow. I would have to learn sales, he insisted, but I would be learning sales on his terms.

What was I thinking? It was 1988, and just a few months earlier the Dow lost 22.6% of its worth in a single day – the infamous "Black Monday." This was more than it had lost in the famous crash of 1929! I was giving up a job in the nation's capital, and for what? My mentor may have owned an FM radio station in the larger city of Portland, but he wanted me to "hit the street" as a new sales rep for his AM station in the town of Lewiston, Maine. Most of the textile and shoe mills were closing, most blue collar jobs were moving off-shore, and the local market was on the verge of collapse!

But it only got worse. I was about to sell good-ole AM radio exclusively in a media world that was already seething with a new, "disruptive innovation." No, I don't mean the internet. This was twenty years ago, and nobody had a computer back then. As for cell phones, that was still a dream. When I called from my desk, I actually had to dial! The disruptive innovation I'm talking about was the growing popularity of FM radio, which was sure to change people's listening habits. Yes, there's a sucker born every minute, and I can pinpoint my exact moment.

If this scenario reminds you in any way of the world you are experiencing now, then I have done my job. Even with cell phones, computers, and the internet, little has really changed. You see, I am still using the very same methods of B2B selling that I learned then, amid the turmoil of twenty years ago. Back then I actually succeeded in building a strong customer base that continued to increase spending (even in tough economic times) on my technologically-challenged product. In fact, I actually doubled my income in that very first year.

Let's fast forward twenty years to today. I now run one of the most successful sales training consulting firms in the media industry, with over 300 clients worldwide! Most of my clients are newspapers, which are experiencing very similar challenges because of the latest "disruptive innovation": the internet and the worldwide web. When you factor in the current economy, you have what some call a "perfect storm." In fact, newspaper ad revenues are showing the sharpest decline in decades![1] How, then, is it even possible that my company's sales methods, now used by hundreds of newspapers, are resulting

---

1   The numbers speak for themselves. According to *Editor & Publisher*, which covers trends in the newspaper industry, total print and online ad revenues for American newspapers fell 12.8% in the first quarter of 2008, as compared to the previous year, the largest decline since the journal began measuring ad results! The steepest decline was in classified advertising, which plummeted by 25% (largely due to websites like Craig's List™), retail advertising plunged by 8.4% and national advertising by 9.5%. For more information, see Jennifer Saba. "Total Newspaper Advertising Continued Steep Descent in Q1 2008," in *Editor & Publisher*, June 18, 2008.

in millions of dollars of new revenue for my clients? Has the storm magically leapfrogged over me?

No. The answer is much simpler than that. All I really do is weave those exact same B2B concepts that I learned from my mentor in the late 1980s into every sales strategy I deploy today. And I do this even though most of the media sales solutions that we design, train on, and take to the street are among the most technically advanced media sales solutions that were ever created.

You see, everything I learned back then still applies today. To survive in B2B sales, you must have B2B skills. By now you must have figured out that when I say B2B, I mean "Business to Business." After all, that's what my consulting firm specializes in. You'd be right, of course, but you still would have missed the second – and in my opinion, the more important – meaning of B2B. It's all about going Back to Basics!

Teaching the same techniques that I learned in the late 1980s has kept me on tour for past two years, or half a million miles, whichever is actually longer. In that time I've conducted workshops for some of the top media companies around the world. I've actually enjoyed hearing my "Street Fighter Workshops Series" being translated into multiple languages, because no matter how strange and exotic they sounded to my American ear, I knew that all those high-priced translators were speaking the exact same words I learned twenty years earlier, before they could even translate terms like page views, click-through rate, cost per click, or geo/behaviorally targeted inventory – because none of those things existed! The words I preach about the basic skills necessary to survive in sales are all about going back to the basics. One plus one still equals two, regardless of whether you use a pen and paper or a laptop. Rapport plus ascertainment still equals sales regardless of whether you're selling in the print edition of a local newspaper or on that newspaper's website.

So it's not the amazing new technologies that are putting a kink in the cogs of sales. But since most people need a scapegoat, let's consider the current economy.

It's a fact: the economy *is* getting tougher by the day. In fact, as I write this chapter, the economy is tanking in worse ways than anyone remembers since the Great Depression. You would think that salespeople would be the first to suffer. After all, who wants to buy the latest gadget when it's hard enough to pay the monthly mortgage? Who wants to invest in an innovative ad campaign when there are hardly any customers left? Before you read on, I owe it to you to be perfectly clear: I love selling in a down economy!

"What?" you're probably wondering out loud. "How can you, Mike Blinder, with twenty years of sales experience, actually love selling in an economy like this? Especially you, a specialist in media advertising sales, when the media is going through such dramatic upheaval and traditional newspaper readership is in a tailspin! What's there to love about a down economy when newspaper ad revenues are actually showing the sharpest decline in decades? That must affect your business!"

The answer is easy. I love a challenge, and a down economy offers exactly that. In some ironic, Darwinian twist, it's a chance for us to thin the herd and weed out the Willy Lomans of the sales world – to let the best and brightest show their mettle. It's a chance to see who's ready to fight to close that deal, because in a down economy, sales really is about fighting for the close – against your competitors and against your own demons.

At a time when only the best survive, this is a chance to show how much you really understand your industry. Every day I ask myself: will newspapers go the way of Polaroid™, and will magazines follow the railroad to oblivion? Sales are a large part of the answer, but first salespeople must understand what it is they're selling. Here's a hint. It's not a product. Polaroid failed because it was selling pictures, not photography. The movie industry dominated the 1940s, but because it sold films instead of entertainment, it soon found itself competing against television and now, video games. Both Polaroid and the movie industry were selling products, not solutions, and that may have been the biggest mistake these industries ever made.

A down economy is really a chance for salespeople to show off their problem-solving skills. Sure there's less money to go around, but that never means that there are fewer needs. People still need cars to get their kids to school. People still need food and clothes, and they even need to know the latest news. As for businesses, rather than giving up in frustration, they need to draw in more customers and drum up more revenue. More than ever, they need to be efficient and overcome those little problems that could once be swept under the rug. They need help, and that's what we, as salespeople, do: we help! With sales, we offer customized (from the word *customer*) solutions to make this economy bearable for everyone, whether it's a homeowner or the manager of a small business. People need help now more than ever. People need us![2]

Of course, this doesn't mean that every salesperson is going to make it through a down economy. The survivors will be people who've honed their skills and realized that there is more to sales than chatting up the customer over martinis or a game of golf. The survivors will be people who understand that sales must be a fulltime profession, which demands certain carefully honed skills. They know that the mathematics of sales go far beyond calculating profit margins.

That's what this book is all about. It's an overview of those basic skills, with tips about how you can make them your own. It's based on the experience I have garnered during more than twenty years in sales, through good economies and bad. Regardless of the state of gas prices and mortgages, two questions always ran through my head as I went out to drum up business:

---

2   And our products need us too. Imagine where Polaroid might be today if it listened to its sales team and started selling photographic solutions, instead of just film!

- How can I offer a tailor-made solution to help my client solve a specific problem?

- What do I need to do to make that close?

After twenty years of constantly selling and closing, I feel compelled to share what I learned. That's what this book is all about.

We've Got the Butter!

There's a famous, if apocryphal, story about a U.S. senator who attended one of those fancy dinners that Washington is known for. While sitting at his table, waiting for the speeches, a waiter came around and placed a pat of butter on everybody's dinner plate. "I'll take two please," the senator said.

"I'm sorry, sir, but I'm afraid there may not be enough."

"But I'd really like some extra butter," the senator answered.

"I understand that sir, and I'd be happy to give you some, but let me make sure that everyone else gets first."

"Do you know who I am?" the senator chuckled. "I'm a U.S. Senator. I chair this committee and that committee and even ran for President," launching into a long list of his many notable achievements.

But the waiter was more annoyed than intimidated: "Do you know who I am, sir? I'm the kid with the butter."

That waiter would have made a great salesperson. No matter how entitled the Senator felt, this young waiter realized that he had one thing that even a powerful Washington bigwig didn't. He had the butter. He had the solution to the Senator's problem – a craving for those extra calories – and he knew that for one brief moment he was in the position of power. There was a problem. He had the solution. He was entitled to set his terms.

I have no doubt that this brave young waiter wanted to help the Senator. A good salesperson also wants to help, rather than simply push some product that he doesn't really believe in. I like to think that the beauty of sales is that it is about more than just making money – it is about altruism. We help the customer identify his problem, then come up with a solution for it. But there is a degree of entitlement too, because we have the solution that our customers need (though it may take some effort to persuade them of that). If I were rewriting the dictionary today, I'd probably define the term *salesperson* as "an entitled altruist."

Salespeople to Avoid

It takes a certain kind of person to really succeed in sales. Or to go back to how I opened this book, in a down economy like this one, some salespeople will succeed while others will fail. It's easy to distinguish between the two.

The salespeople who will succeed are the ones who aren't just in it for the buck. They have a genuine desire to help other people by identifying their problems and coming up with original solutions. At the same time though, they recognize that this ability to help others actually entitles them to do so. It's okay to be rewarded for your efforts, which is why sales can be so lucrative. After all, the more you help, the more you should be rewarded.

On the other hand there are plenty of people who come to sales with the wrong attitude. No matter how much they try to fight the odds, these people are destined to fail, especially in a down economy. If you're trying to figure out who's who, there are three types of salespeople to be wary of:

In *Death of a Salesman* Arthur Miller casts Willy Loman as the anti-salesman par excellence: the kind of guy who will lose everything. "Be liked and you will never want," he advises his sons. In other words, "I like people and people like me; I would be a perfect salesman." Wrong! Salesmen are not there to make friends. Salespeople are there to solve problems, and sometimes that can be painful. "No pain, no gain," is as true in sales as it is in exercise. Would you trust a doctor who talked more about his golf game, and avoided giving you a diagnosis because you may not like what you hear? How will a salesperson who acts like that deal with rejection, regardless of the reason? "But I thought you were my friend, so why won't you buy from me?" just won't cut it in a down economy. The "friend" is not the kind of salesperson who will make it.

"Never trust the artist; trust the tale," said D.H. Lawrence, and this applies doubly to sales. So to all those people who claim that "my friends say I'm a natural salesman," I have one thing to say: "It's not about you." Sales demand nurture, not nature. So let's move away from that phony assumption that it takes a certain charisma to sell. It takes practice and a set of skills, and these have to be refined over time. People will buy when they believe in what you offer, and they'll only believe in what you offer when it's exactly what they need. As for those who think that personal charisma and charm will carry them home to the close, ask yourself: would you trust the class clown just because he is funny?

Finally, "I know the product inside out!" is one of the worst reasons to get into sales. Most people who need a word processor and Internet aren't really interested in all the intricate details of one particular motherboard or another. That's why computer geeks are some of the most awful salespeople that I've ever met. In fact, back in 1995, when the internet was first getting started, the idea that the best experts are often the worst salesmen hit home.

I knew nothing about the internet back then, and wasn't even sure that it would take off. But still, I was willing to take a gamble, so I quit my job and joined the staff of the *Portland Press Herald* in Portland, Maine, to start their internet advertising division. I soon had a meeting with the Freeport Merchants Association, which includes such huge businesses as L.L. Bean, and realized that the time had come for me to learn how to actually get on line. So I lugged my shiny new computer into the office of a local service provider and hoped for the best. I didn't get it. Instead the owner, an obnoxious kid in cut-off shorts, grilled me about my new desktop. He hated it, and had a checklist of everything that was wrong with it. In fact, he actually seemed bothered that I would even try to drive my new jalopy on his own personal information super-highway. But the worst part was when he asked, rather rudely, what I possibly needed the internet for. When I told him about my new job with the *Press Herald* and my meeting with the Merchants Association, he snickered and said, "Don't even bother. I already have their account." My old job started looking a lot more attractive. There was no way I could compete as a novice with that geeky whiz kid.

But I'm never one to give up. I got on the internet and played around, and kept my appointment two weeks later. But when I walked through the door, I told them upfront about my hesitations: "I think I may be wasting your time," I said. "I do work for a large media company, but there's no way I could possibly compete with that *gentleman* in Portland who knows everything there is to know about the web." I spoke too soon. "Who, him?" the executive director answered, "I never understand a word he says." That's when it really hit home: it's not what you know; it's what the customer needs. By now you should also know that the self-described "expert" is yet another salesperson who will not make it in a down economy.

Some Things to Think About

Before you go on reading this book, ask yourself the following questions:

- Do you want to help people?

- Do you deserve to be rewarded for a job well done?

- Can you speak to people in their own language?

- Are you willing to work at your skills to get the best results for you and your clients?

If you answered yes to these four questions, then it doesn't matter if you have an MBA or a degree in Marine Biology like I do. You have what it takes to be a successful salesperson in the world of B2B sales, and I'm excited to help you get you there.

Attention All Managers!

In some businesses sales managers are people who rise through the ranks of sales. Most of them will know what I'm talking about, intellectually or instinctively, so for them this book is just a refresher, or a chance to put some ideas into words.

But other businesses, including several media firms I've encountered, tend to promote their finest people from other departments to manage their sales team. Unfortunately, some of their past experiences may cause them to push a different approach than the tried and true one necessary in sales. In fact, I actually remember someone who lacked true "street experience" but had recently been put in charge of sales nonetheless suggesting that my approach was too "aggressive" ... when dealing with a used car salesman! Too often it's these kinds of managers who slow down the sales effort.

So even if you are a manager, this book could be for you. Sales is an art but it is also a science, and in some ways its techniques are different – in some ways they are *very* different – from what you may be used to. I believe this book will help you understand your customers, but perhaps more importantly, it will help you help the people you supervise and who look to you for guidance.

Chapter I

It's a Numbers Game

I am not judged by the number of times I fail, but by the number of times I succeed: and the number of times I succeed is in direct proportion to the number of times I fail and keep trying.

—Tom Hopkins

Telemarketers tend to have the toughest assignment in sales. They call hundreds of people every day, and get hung up on most of the time. They are insulted or abused more than any other type of salesperson! So why do they do it? Not the telemarketers themselves: we know why they do it. They're part-time workers — retirees and college kids — trying to pay the rent, and maybe put a little aside. But why do businesses invest so much money in teams of telemarketers working round the clock? The answer is obvious. Because it works!

According to the Direct Marketing Association (2004), the telephone, as intrusive as it is, was more than three and a half times as successful a marketing tool for show marketers than direct mail and email combined![1] Of course, the real numbers are not very high, averaging about 6 percent, but given the amount of calls made, those numbers add up. If 100 calls a day lead to six closes, then 1,000 calls a day could be more than enough to keep you in business.

In fact, most of us get similar results. How many closes do you

---

[1] This is based on the DMA's 2004 Response Rate Report, which claimed a 7.18% response rate for telemarketers, as opposed to just 1.23% for direct mail to homes, and 0.85% for email. For direct order campaigns, the response rate was slightly lower (5.78%), but still double the combined rates of the other top methods: 3-dimensional mailings, such as promotional items (2.3%) and catalogs (2.18%).

get from each prospect? In media sales – the world that I know best – if you have 20 prospects on your list, 10 of them are worth your time; of these, 5 will get you to someone to talk to, and of those 5, about 3 will deserve an actual proposal. Of those 3, you can usually close with one. In other words, for every twenty prospects you list, you are likely to close just one. The rest is simple math. If your ratio of sales to prospects is 1:20, it is roughly the same of the telemarketers! The biggest difference is that they probably make a lot more calls than you do!

Are you starting to feel like you're in the wrong business? Don't! There are two easy ways to raise your numbers. The first is to go out and get more prospects; the second is to get your closing ratio higher. Both these steps are essential to sales, especially in a down economy. The first thing a sales survivor must do is get those numbers up! You always need to raise the ratio of successful closes to prospects, but even before that, you need to get the number of prospecting calls that you make up. In a down economy, when people are fighting just to keep their numbers on par, how do you go about doing that?

Always Want More!

The numbers that I used above seem about right for most salespeople. They should, because I took actual

> *"I'm a great believer in luck, and find the more I work the more I have of it."*
> — Thomas Jefferson

numbers for media sales that we analyzed right here at the Blinder Group. Are they the right numbers for you? Do you even know what your close-to-prospect ratio is? Do you know how many prospecting calls you make each day, and what kind of results you get from them?

Don't be upset by these questions. Plenty of salespeople don't know their ratios, whether it's per day, per month, or per quarter. So the first thing that you need to do is to figure out your ratios and calculate exactly what kind of results you're getting. The best way to do this is by using a spreadsheet. While some people like to keep track in their head, it's amazing how much more meaningful these numbers are when you actually see them in front of you. When they're printed on a spreadsheet in black and white, there's absolutely no way you can fudge them around.

In most cases, your boss will expect you to keep track of your calls. If that isn't the case, you can still do it yourself by making a spreadsheet and keeping a record of what actually takes place during each call you make, whether electronically, on the phone, or in person. While sales is a numbers game, what we're counting is *actions*, not just the amount of times that you pick up the receiver and dial a number, or get in your car and drive to meet a customer.

Every call can consist of one or more (hopefully more) of the following five distinct types of actions:

- **Prospecting:** This is the one we all dread: sifting through countless businesses to find the golden leads. Essentially, this is what telemarketing is all about. Telemarketers make hundreds of more or less random calls until they find someone who's even slightly interested, and then they often turn them over to a professional salesperson. By the end of this chapter though, you'll realize that a sales survivor has one great advantage over the average telemarketer: we've taken the term *random* out of the equation.

- **Ascertainment:** This action is essential to determine what your customers really need (more on that later). While everyone realizes how important this is when speaking to new prospects, what too many salespeople forget is that ascertainment is just as important with longtime customers who may have new or changing needs that must also be addressed.

- **The Pitch:** This is the actual mechanics of sales – the very essence of selling – the specific actions that you take to excite your prospects about buying your product. For some salespeople, however, the pitch can be almost as difficult as prospecting. Hopefully, by the end of this book, they'll realize that it's actually as easy as ABC … literally!

- **The Close:** This is the one we've all been waiting for: the deal is clinched and you are exchanging products or services for dollars and cents. In fact, all of the previous steps should be leading up to The Close, because this is what sales is all about.

- **Service:** Sales doesn't end with the Close though. Remember that it takes more energy to find a new customer than to keep a regular customer happy so that he keeps coming back to you for all his future needs. For many salespeople, solving all the customer's little problems can actually be the easiest part of the job. After all, what can be more relaxing and enjoyable than schmoozing with a satisfied customer and making sure that they are getting the best out of the product you just sold them? Of course, one of the hardest things we sometimes have to do is to train those customers who love to entangle us with their laborious conversations that we really do have lots of work to do, and we can't spend hours chatting away with them.

Now, with all this in mind, ask yourself how many *actions* – and not just calls – have you actually made today? How many service *actions* did you make to help an existing client, and how many prospecting *actions* did you make, whether to introduce yourself to new business prospects or to see if any of your existing customers can be sold new products or services? Finally, how many of your *actions* were to actually ask for the order?

There is, however, one dangerous trap that many salespeople fall into. Far too often they tend to think of each call having a single purpose. Absolutely not! In fact, every single call you make can include one or all of the other actions. When you make a service call, you can ask your customer if she knows anyone else who may be interested in that product (*prospecting*) or see if he has other needs (*ascertainment*). You might decide to try *pitching* a new product, and because your customers trust you, they decide to go ahead and place an order (*closing*). This is just one plausible example, so remember, when updating your spreadsheet, count your actions, not your calls!

On that same note, another common mistake that salespeople make is that they prefer to focus more on service than on vital prospecting actions. The reason is obvious: providing service is so much easier. Every one of us has an innate desire to take the easy road and travel the paths that we know best. Remember though that no road is harder than the "easy road" – at least that's what I've always found. So ask yourself, are you really getting more business that way? Is it really improving your numbers? "To thine own self be true."[2]

Using your spreadsheet, figure out exactly how many of your calls really are about prospecting, then set yourself goals to get that number higher. When I work with media companies, I insist that each and every one of their salespeople targets twenty new prospects each week, regardless of what else they're doing. You can insist on this for yourself too. And don't go easy on yourself with your goals either: As the golfer Jason Tyska once said: "When you set a goal, you want to make it hard on yourself." You won't always hit a hole in one, but you won't be any less the salesperson for trying.

And prospecting really isn't as hard as it sounds.

---

2   William Shakespeare, *Hamlet*, Act I, Scene III.

Drawing Bull's-eyes

The more people you call, the more sales you will make. That's plain old common sense. But that doesn't mean you should spend your time

> *"It is far more important to be able to hit the target than it is to haggle over who makes a weapon or who pulls the trigger."*
> — Dwight D. Eisenhower

randomly cold calling, like our friends the telemarketers. Your time is valuable and you want to make the most of it, so make sure each of those calls counts! The best way to do that is to find your market niche.

That should be obvious to anyone, but more often than not, it isn't. Even the best salespeople don't target their potential markets specifically enough. Of course, a man selling fine Kobe beef is not going to target a list of vegan restaurants, but is he considering the economic demographic of the local supermarket? Is a middle class family with a mortgage and five kids to put through college really ready to buy a Ferrari? Yet how many car salesmen go on and on about how great the stereo system is, when they're trying to push a car to the parents of a brood of teenagers?

Salespeople often pitch first, then call whatever they hit their target. I see this all too often in the media business. It's so common to launch new products that I often joke with media sales reps: "How many special sections do you have deadlining today?" Don't get me wrong! Those special sections are great, but they lose their edge if the salespeople call the same old customers over and over again. That's why I'm constantly reminding them to boil down exactly who each new product targets. It's a lot easier than it sounds. In fact, the target can easily be boiled down to four specific groups:

- Young or Old;
- Rich or Poor;
- Near or Far;
- Man or Woman.

Once you know who each special section targets, you will be far more likely to find just the right advertisers for that section – and just as importantly, know who to put on hold until you have something more appropriate for them. In other words, in a down economy sales survivors are the ones who know exactly who they are targeting their products for.

So don't be like the proverbial archer practicing in the woods. With his arms proudly folded across his chest, he's eager to show every passer-by that each of his arrows has hit a bull's-eye. Of course, what he fails to explain is that first he shot the arrow, and only then did he paint a bull's-eye around it. Truly skilled archers (and salespeople) pick their targets first!

You don't know me but ...

If, after you've targeted your potential prospects, you find yourself running out of "low-hanging fruit," don't

> *"In sales a referral is the key to the door of resistance."*
> — Bo Bennett

be afraid to ask your best customers if they know any potential new prospects for you. It's amazing what you can get when you ask, so go ahead and ask them: "I know you're really pleased with my product. Is there anyone else that you think would want it?" I've always found that satisfied customers are eager to share that kind of information, especially if they really are happy with the product you've sold them. If they believe in it as much as you do, they can easily become your greatest advocates.

So get those names from them and name drop: "I was talking to your friend Sue, and she suggested I give you a call. Actually, it's more than just name dropping. It's a personal recommendation and borrowed trust.

Chapter 1

Contacts, Contacts Everywhere ...

The amazing thing about potential new leads is that with a little ingenuity, you can find them just about everywhere!

> *"Who seeks shall find."*
> — Sophocles

Hindu scriptures talks of two sleepless sages: Alert and Watchful, ever vigilant and ever searching. While I may not want to be sleepless like them, I do try to imitate their vigilance, so wherever I am, no matter what I am doing, I am always on the lookout for new leads. "Ask, and it shall be given you; seek, and ye shall find; knock, and it shall be opened unto you" (Matthew 7:7).

Once you realize how many leads there really are out there, you'll soon want to carry a pen and pad with you just about everywhere you go. You never know who you'll meet in the waiting room of your dentist's office, at your kid's recital, or at the dinner party that you couldn't squirm out of. Of course, there are some places where that might not be particularly appropriate. In most churches that I know, for instance, the congregation tends to frown upon people who start discussing business during the sermon. Still, the contacts are there, so if someone really catches your attention, make a mental note of it, and jot the relevant information down when you "run to the restroom."

As a sales manager, I always asked my team when they came back from their meetings if they dropped off their cards at all the neighboring businesses. This can be especially appropriate for salespeople targeting certain industries that are often clustered together. Car dealerships are a classic example, but have you ever noticed how your favorite restaurant is usually located near several other restaurants in an "entertainment district"? In other words, there are plenty of other businesses on that same block that may need your professional assistance! Strip malls are another great place to prospect, especially for business-to-business sales.[3] So the next time you are dragged out shopping, take a few extra business cards with you – by now you should realize that you must always have a stack on hand – and hand them out wherever you go.

At this point, I'm already assuming that you've taken the "left-right rule" to heart, and

> *"Opportunities multiply as they are seized."*
> — Sun Tzu

notice all the businesses to the left and right of the one you are calling on (and to the left and right of the streets leading up to it). You've already staked out your territory, so now you need to find some new grounds to conquer.

Why not try leaving for your meeting 15 minutes earlier and take a new route to get there. It could even be just five blocks over, down that street you try to avoid because of all the traffic lights. Remember, traffic lights mean traffic, so there's probably plenty of traffic there too. What kind of businesses are down that street? Do you have the perfect solutions for them? If you think about it, there are plenty of ways to get to where you're going, and in sales, all roads do, indeed, lead to prospects!

Finally, two words about national leads groups: "Hate 'em!" They're a waste of money, and you can find leads on your own with much better results. On the other hand, I do love getting together with top B2B sales reps, each of them product exclusive (and obviously not competing with me!). For example, I am in media advertising, but once a month I get together for breakfast with the best and brightest salespeople in commercial real estate, auto leasing, office supplies, computer networking, as well as the infamous copier sales person. Over coffee and French toast we all share leads. In fact, our group is in such demand that if someone

---

3   But not the great indoor shopping malls that dot the American landscape. Shops in strip malls are usually run by the owners themselves, whereas stores in large shopping malls generally belong to local or nationwide chains. Apart from some basic hiring and firing, on-site managers usually have very little say in the decision-making process for their businesses. In sales you must speak to the real decision-makers.

doesn't consistently bring the same number of leads that the rest of us are bringing, there are dozens of competitors out there eager to replace him (and in fact, fresh blood does invigorate the group). So put together your own B2B leads group with a diverse assortment of product-exclusive salespeople like yourself. Not only will you get new leads from them; you may also get plenty of new ideas. No less important: a little camaraderie with like-minded salespeople in the morning is bound to boost the rest of your day!

And don't ignore your competition either. When I work with local newspapers, I insist that their salespeople check the local media religiously to see who's advertising with them, because that's the most obvious sign that a company has advertising needs. When training new reps one of my basic tenets is that they must always listen to different radio stations when driving to a sales meeting to find out which potential new prospects are advertising on those stations. See which local businesses are advertising on CNN and other major television networks. Who has ads on the local news station or in the movie theater right before the feature? What ads do you see on billboards and buses, or when you turn on your computer to visit local websites? Just make sure you have your pad and pen handy to jot down all their names.

According to David Shenk, the average American was exposed to 560 advertising messages a day in 1971, but this number increased to over 3,000 in 1997, i.e., ten years ago, before the boom in internet advertising,[4] and is already at 5,000 today.[5] This means that each and every one of us is exposed to over 1.8 million ads a year. If prospecting is all about searching for gold, it doesn't matter whether you're selling media advertising like me, or paper clips or office furniture. You just struck a goldmine that's been staring you right in the face!

In a nutshell, what I'm trying to say is this: Prospecting opportunities are out there, even in those places you most dread going to – so take some business cards along, and start doing the prospecting circuit.

4   See David Shenk., *Data Smog: Surviving the Information Glut.* Harper Edge, 1997.
5   Belden Associates, 2008.

Just remember what Sun Tzu said: "A thousand battles are a thousand victories," and in B2B survival sales, we're all about victories!

Business Cards

Sales can never be a nine-to-five job. We're always meeting people, and we're

> *"Don't agonize, organize!"*
> — Florynce R. Kennedy

always making contacts, whether it's on the job, at church, or at a PTA meeting. Based on everything I said above, by the end of each day, you should end up with dozens of new contacts, each represented by a handy-dandy business card. Pretty soon, your wallet will be bulging, with the overflow vying for space in your pockets! It's almost impossible to keep track of them all!

That's why, when I get home or back to my hotel after a long day of meetings, like most of you I empty my pockets. In my case I usually find three separate "stashes" of business cards. I learned years ago to "load" my own cards in one of my pockets, where they are easily accessible (in my case, my right-hand jacket pocket). Then I put the ones that I receive over the course of the day in one of two other pockets. The cards that I can honestly say will require little or no action on my part, except maybe inclusion in my contact list, will usually end up in my left-hand jacket pocket. However, the most promising ones that I have been given (or the ones that I specifically asked for) can always be found in the breast pocket of my shirt (close to my heart). This is also where I keep the little slips of paper where I jot down new leads and personal information about people without business cards. What I have is a stash of information containing all the crucial contacts that require some near-term action: a follow-up e-mail or phone call, delivery on a promise to provide some information, or possibly research I need to do in order to learn more about these prospect and eventually to "pitch" them some business.

How do I remember who's who? Having the usual post-fifty

memory lapses, I found a creative way around that challenge. Instead of just collecting the business cards, I take a minute to look at them, and sometimes I will even comment on them to the prospect: "I like the design! Who made it for you?" And always, always, I'll jot down a little note to tell me something about the person who gave it to me. It could be as simple as "Top decision-maker. Call Wednesday. Send a proposal." The absolutely essential cards in the pack – the Babe Ruths of baseball cards in the business world – are the ones that I mark the most simply, with two exclamation points: !! They're also the easiest for me to find the next morning, because I keep them on my night stand or stuck into my keyboard, to make sure that they are my first priority. As for the other cards, I'll remember who they are just by looking at the note.

There is another advantage to this too. People notice when I comment on the card or scribble a little note. To them I'm not just one more person who happens to have their business card. I'm the guy that took an interest!

Turning the Corner

With your list of prospects ready, it's time for you to attack. But before you do that, let's be perfectly clear! No prospect, no matter what business they're in, has the time to give you an unscheduled 30 or 40 minutes so that you can learn about their needs. In fact, it's actually insulting to them to even assume that they could give you that time, because what you're really suggesting is that they have all the free time in the world. And it's insulting to you too, because the prospect will wonder what kind of professional you are if you have all that free time for unscheduled appointments.

That's why your initial cold-call prospecting, whether on the phone or in person, should take no more than 4 or 5 minutes, during which you appear as busy as possible. Your mission is simple: you want to come away with the following information:

- Who is the decision-maker?

- Who influences the decisions?

- How do these decision-makers prefer to be contacted?

Finally, and most important of all: you're there to get a firm appointment set up so that you can sit down with the prospect face-to-face or have a lengthier phone conversation to ascertain his goals and needs. So, in short, if you're prospecting on the phone, make sure to sound very, very busy. If you're prospecting face-to-face, make it seem as if you only have a few seconds. I'll talk more about that later.

The Elevator Statement

Now that you know how to find the prospects, you have to know what to say to them.

> *"Brevity is a great charm of eloquence."*
> — Cicero

Remember that these people are busy, or at least they like to tell you they are, so they probably have very little time to listen to you. That is why you must make sure you have your elevator statement down pat.

For those of you not in the know, an elevator statement is a brief, carefully worded statement about your business. It tells your prospect exactly what you do, with all the benefits and none of the pain. It's called an elevator statement because you should be able to recite the whole thing in the time it takes you to ride an elevator for a total of ten floors. In other words, you have to cram all that information into just 30 seconds!

Now, I am not a believer in scripts. As a former radio deejay and television talent, it should be apparent that I love to ad lib. But even I have written scripted elevator statements describing all the benefits of my business. I call them my "Wow! statements," because at the end of them, I expect my listeners to respond with a "Wow!" even if it's something they don't usually think about. To test a new elevator statement, I like to try it out at cocktails parties to see what kind of response it elicits. While I include the obvious in my statement ("As you may know ..."), I'll cap it off with something new and exciting that few people know about my business: "What you may not know is ..." And always craft it the exact same way: Benefit, benefit, benefit ... *and no pain!*

For example, "My name is Mike Blinder. As you may know I founded and manage the Blinder Group, an innovative sales training and consulting firm. What you may not know is that this year we helped generated over $45 million of guaranteed new revenue for our clients from new advertiser categories, achieving over 55 percent closing ratios, and we did that *very* cost-effectively for our clients!"

Of course, the best way to get that "Wow!" is to actually believe in what you're saying. The internet is full of helpful sites to help you craft an elevator statement, but the best elevator statements do *not* follow some formula or other about vocabulary, structure, or the number of words. The best statements are the most sincere statements, and the most sincere statements are the ones you believe in with all your heart and all your soul. So craft your elevator statement assiduously. Rehearse it regularly, in front of the mirror or in front of your friends. But remember, it's also called a "Wow! statement." I like to think that this is not only because it wows the pants off your prospects, but also because, if you listen to it closely, it will wow the pants off of you! If it doesn't, you may as well quit your job!

Huh? That's right, because the people I've met who have the most problems crafting elevator statements are the ones who have lost faith in the product their selling (I'm working on the optimistic assumption that the ones who never believed in it in the first place aren't actually trying to sell it). Just remember one simple thing: we're not all Sally Field or Dustin Hoffman. We don't have countless Oscar nominations for our prolific acting careers. In other words, our customers will know right away whether we truly believe in our product ... or not. So if you've really lost faith in your product, then learn more about it or find yourself a mentor. And if it still doesn't work for you, then fix it!

But if, after all that sincere effort, after all that soul-searching, you still can't bring yourself to believe that what you are selling will really benefit the prospect you're pitching it to, then maybe it's time to start finding another job. In short, you're not that good of an actor.

Toys to Play With

As the father of a young child, I have learned what every parent knows: kids love new toys ... for exactly

> *"The people are a very fickle baby that must have new toys every day."*
> — Emma Goldman

ten seconds. Then they discover the magic of the box it came in! Adults love new toys too, and business people are no exception. So when you're out there prospecting, make sure you mention your shiniest new toy – the one you're bringing them for the very first time – directly after your Wow! statement. "I know how busy you are, but the reason for this interruption is that this week we launched an exciting program that I believe could very well be a great match for a business like yours!"

Get right into the razzle and the dazzle of your shiny new toy, as soon as you finish your elevator statement: "This is who I am (*elevator*), and this is something hot off the presses that I think might be of benefit to you!" (*shiny toy*). In fact, I believe that this is so essential that if by chance you don't have a shiny toy to dangle in front of your prospect's face, make one up! Find a product that your customer doesn't know about, but that you think could be a perfect fit and dangle it, swing it, clang it, and bang it, just as if you were dangling an old set of keys in front of a mesmerized baby. It's quite possible that your customer will act just like that baby and try to grab the keys. It's a natural reflex. We're programmed that way. But don't leave all your cookies on the counter. The purpose of the shiny toy is to spark their interest and get them to give you permission to pursue.

In fact, I'm convinced that it's all these shiny toys, some of them without any immediate value, that quickly become the market staple. I remember when cars had roll-up windows, with a manual crank that you had to turn just to get the window down. Were automatic windows really a necessity for a nation that exercised way too much, since they helped them save those precious calories by not having to crank? Or were they just a shiny new toy that car salespeople could add to their growing list of features: "Now with all-new power windows!" I can actually hear those old commercials in my head, and wonder if anyone would even consider buying a car with a window crank today.

Sun Tzu realized that shiny new toys are critical to success in warfare, but what he wrote is just as relevant to success in sales: "Hold out baits to entice your enemy!" Shiny toys are your baits, because shiny toys really do sell! That is why, when you meet with your prospect, make sure you have your shiniest toys right up front where they can dazzle him as soon as you're done with your elevator statement.

There is another advantage to shiny toys too. They offer a ready-made explanation as to why you decided to call on this prospect, ostensibly from out of the blue. No one wants to be disturbed, least of all busy businesspeople. With a shiny new toy you have an excuse, not only to interrupt, but to interrupt now.

Who's the Boss?

Assuming that you're feeling comfortable with finding new prospects and breaking the ice, there's only one

> *"Sell to the organ-grinder, not to the monkey."*
> — Alan Cymberg

thing left to figure out: who do you actually speak to? Basically, there's one rule of thumb: "Sell to the organ grinder, not to the monkey!" Always make sure that the person you're talking to is the decision-maker, rather than just some random underling who likes to play the chief. In fact, your goal should be to discover, not only who the decision-makers are, but who influences the decision-makers too.

A few years ago, while I was traveling, someone called my office, insisting on speaking only to me. With a major conference just a few days away, he had to get the final advertisements into the program, and he wanted me to buy one. When Robin, who answered the office phone, asked if she could possibly help or even take a message for me, Jack on the other end was downright rude to her: "No, I'll only speak to Mike. I want you to tell me how I can contact him now!" Despite Robin's requests for more information, Jack kept insisting, "I'll only speak to Mike," and eventually left a telephone number for me to call him back.

What poor Jack didn't realize then was that Robin is not only someone who happened to pick up the phone that day. She is also my business partner, and the person at the Blinder Group who writes all the checks. Worst of all, he didn't realize that Robin is not only my business partner/check-writer: she is also my wife!

So, a few hours later, when I got the email from Robin with Jack's message, she added one important note: "Don't you dare buy anything from that bozo! And if you do, don't expect me to write the check!" Now, I may have been planning to buy an ad, but given the circumstances, what choice did I have?

That's why I always warn people that before they even set foot in a business, they must try to find out who the decision-makers are. Actually, they should also find out who the people who influence decisions are. The best way to do this is simply to ask. Call the businesses that you're prospecting and ask whoever answers who makes the decisions. At one time I had the receptionist at my radio station do it between reading tabloids and filing her nails. During her abundant downtime, I had her call each of the potential prospects I had generated for the week. She told them that she was updating our files and needed to know who the decision-makers were. That way, the next time I called, I could always get past the "gate keeper" by asking to speak to the decision-maker directly. And trust me, you will get a lot farther by asking to speak to Bill Smith directly than by asking to speak to some random person in charge of making advertising decisions.

Today, some companies I work with use telemarketers to do this: not to sell, but to collect information. With a list of potential prospects in front of them, these telemarketers will call up and give each business a grade, based on the information they managed to glean:

- **C:** They know who the decision-maker is.

- **B:** They actually spoke to the decision-maker.

- **A:** The decision-maker is "hot to trot" and the telemarketer already set up a meeting for me!

Is it worth the extra money? Sure, because each of these calls saves valuable time for the sales reps.

And when you do get around to setting up that meeting, ask that all the relevant decision-makers are at that meeting too. I learned this in my first year of sales, when I prospected the president of a bank about 50 miles away. Of course, my mentor had trained me to ask that all the decision-makers be present, but I was intimidated by the audacity of the request. When I finally had the ban president on the phone and got him to agree to a meeting two weeks later to discuss his advertising and marketing needs, I was tempted to stop there. But then I remembered my mentor instructions, and worked up the courage to say the following, just as I had been trained to do. "I know your time is important and so is mine. Since we will be discussing advertising and marketing do you think it would be possible to have the people who assist you in making these decisions attend this meeting too?" There was a long pause, and I began to contemplate how badly I had insulted him. In fact, I began to wonder whether he had hung up on me.

Finally, he broke the silence. "Mike," he said, is that your name?

Mike?"

"Yes," I mumbled, dreading what was next.

"If I could get my sales department to ask that question, I bet I would double my billing!"

In the end, I got the account, but even more importantly, I learned a great lesson in how to prospect customers.

The Art of Stealth

The problem is that sometimes it seems downright impossible to get past that ever-vigilant gatekeeper and

> *"TAKE: v.t., to acquire, frequently by force but preferably by stealth.*
> — Ambrose Bierce

speak to the real decision-maker. But as they say, "Desperate times call for desperate measures," and "desperate measures" means stealth. Over the years I've learned a few tricks to circumvent the people circumventing me. Each of them has worked at one time or another, and they are sure to be helpful in a pinch.

The first thing to realize is that gate-keeping is usually a nine-to-five job. The receptionist who sits in front of the boss's desk doesn't usually get paid by the hour or the earning. It is a steady job with a steady salary, and most importantly, steady hours. The decision-maker, on the other hand, usually thinks business around the clock. Since most of their workday is filled with mundane chores and constant interruptions, they'll often be the first to arrive in the morning and/or the last to leave at night. So call then: either early in the morning or late in the evening, after the gatekeepers have left for the day.

I remember how all my efforts to speak to the VP for Marketing at the *Detroit Free Press* were thwarted by his erstwhile receptionist. Since there was no way to get through her, I decided to go around her instead. One morning I took a chance and called the office at 7:05 am. Sure enough, the VP answered the phone himself: after all, he was the only person in the office at that ungodly hour.

Similarly, toward the end of the lunch hour is another excellent time to call. The gatekeeper has usually gone out to eat, leaving the target to fend for himself.

When I first began doing sales, I was left with the dregs from the proverbial barrel of prospects. One of the people I was expected to contact was a man who absolutely refused to speak with me, never mind to meet with me. With all my appeals for a lunch meeting beaten down, I decided to try the next best thing. During my prospecting I had befriended his secretary, and one day she leaked some invaluable information: her boss had brought a bag lunch to work! It was the kind of tip I had long been waiting for! At about the lunch hour I had a pizza delivered to him in his office with a note: "If you won't have lunch *with* me, at least have lunch *on* me! When can we speak?"

Like many good stories, this one has two endings: Later that day I had the empty pizza box delivered to my office via messenger. Inside it was a note that read, "Never." Don't feel bad though, because I said there was a second ending: three months later I got his business, and it was a top account. Persistence pays off.

There are other things you can do as well. If the number on a business card takes you to a combative receptionist, simply switch the last two digits of the phone number and redial. In a large office with an internal phone system, this will usually take you to another employee. Ask that employee to connect you directly. While he may not have the direct number memorized, employees usually have a list of staff phone numbers readily available. Also, with many phone systems the digital display on the decision-maker's phone will appear as an internal call, which is far more likely to be accepted.

The point is that there are plenty of ways to get around those gatekeepers, who are, after all, only doing their job. Sure, they may be intimidating at times, but that's actually the best part of the challenge. Which leaves us with only one thing left to overcome ...

Fear Itself!

So many salespeople are afraid of making that first call. I know I am, and all too often I'll find every

> *"The only thing we have to fear is fear itself."*
> — Franklin Delano Roosevelt

excuse in the book not to do it. "Here I go! I'm about to make that call ... but first I'd better straighten up my desk ... Okay, now I'm ready. I'll just get myself a cup of coffee and I'll do it ... Wait! What if my wife calls in the middle? Maybe I should call her first to tell her that I'll be busy for the next half hour ... There, I've got all my notes out ... Hmmm, is that a typo? I'd better check it ... Whoa! Will you look at that! I have a meeting in ten minutes. Where has the day gone? I can't possibly call now! I guess it will have to wait until tomorrow." Sound familiar?

It should, because just about everyone one of us does it. We're all afraid to take that first step, whether we're talking about a phone call or a face-to-face meeting – and everything I say here holds true for both. I know that I hate making that first call. When I used to drive to new prospecting calls, I could have sworn my car had a mind of its own, because it sometimes refused to make the turn into the prospect's parking lot. The reason for this was quite simple: rejection. No one wants to be rejected! It doesn't matter if it's the pimply kid in high school who's too afraid to ask a date to the prom, or the seasoned sales professional who's afraid of being turned down by the prospect. We all hate to be told, "No!" I admit it. It's my greatest fear too, and the one I work the hardest to overcome.

I'm not the only one who hates it either. Larry Pinci and Phil Glosserman wrote an entire book, *Sell the Feeling*, on how to handle the fear of rejection in sales.[6] One of their key points is that this fear actually comes from salespeople focusing on themselves and their own inadequacies, rather than on the clients and their needs. Everyone,

---

6   Larry Pinci and Phil Glosserman. *Sell the Feeling: The 6-Step System that Drives People to Do Business with You.* Morgan James Publishing, 2008.

especially today, is spoon-fed an idealized image of the world by mass media, like television. As a kid, how often did I wish that my family could be more like the Beaver's, with my mom, just like June Cleaver herself, vacuuming the living room with a freshly starched apron around her pencil-thin waist, and a string of pearls around her neck. Intellectually, we know that this is a fiction, and that Barbara Billingsley made plenty of money to play that role, but emotionally we are still trapped believing that we should be more like the Cleavers, the Bradys, or the Huckstables. We've developed an inferiority complex because of some fictionalized ideal.

Fear might not be internal just to you either. You may be the new kid on the block, completely devoted to your product, but some of the veterans may be more jaded, and actually poison you against it. Too many salespeople just starting out will break all sales records, only to be told by the "inside scoop" by some of their "more experienced" colleagues: the rates are too high, the competition is stiff, no one is buying, and the market is crumbling. These are just some of the signs of impending sales burnout, and while very little has been written about this dangerous phenomenon, it is very real and it is very contagious!

Regardless of whether this fear of rejection stems from your own insecurities or the cynicism implanted in you by your peers, remember what Eleanor Roosevelt said: "No one can make you feel inferior without your consent." We have to conquer fear of rejection, in sales and in life itself, and to quote one of America's greatest businessmen, "If you want to conquer fear, do not sit at home and think about it. Go out and get busy!"[7]

No!

By now you've been speaking with the prospect for just under a minute. Your Wow! statement and shiny toy statement together can be measured in seconds, and ideally, you've emphasized this by your

---

7 Dale Carnegie.

actions. When making a cold call face-to-face, always keep your coat on and check your watch to signal that you don't have lots of time. If you're on the phone, act hurriedly and say that you only have a few seconds (not minutes) to spare.

Still, those few seconds are more than enough time for your prospect, especially a cold-call prospect, to realize that you are a salesperson and that they are "under threat" of possibly buying something. I like to say that I've never been hit, but I have seen prospects show a queasy feeling as that magical, two-letter word forms in their gut, and creeps its way up their spine to their mouths. By just opening their mouths and intoning *No!* they believe they can wish their worries away.

So let them. One old sales technique is to get the prospect to actually say that magic word, just to get it out of the way. According to some of the best old sales trainers, the Wow! statement and shiny toy statement should be followed immediately by a specific question to which the answer is truly *no*. For example, "After hearing this, do you see any reason why I can't ask you three or four very brief questions?"

Nine times out of ten, the prospect will respond with a resounding "No!" and the word is simply out of the way. While he may have tried to hinder your progress, he's suddenly given you permission to pursue. So remember, never be threatened by the word *no*. Embrace it, and turn it to your advantage. To do this you must first remember that when a prospect tells you *no*, he is not actually rejecting you, but his own ability to solve a problem and move forward.

The Survey

Now that the prospect is willing to continue, take your few remaining minutes to find out some very important information that will help you proceed. Ask who actually makes the decisions, who influences them, how to contact that person. Most importantly, get the ascertainment call set up and in your calendar by asking when they think they might have time to discuss the matter at greater length. Your goal is simple:

you want them to grant you thirty or forty minutes, in which you can learn about their goals, needs and desires.

My line of choice has always been, "I have this new product that I think could be a good match. There's no way I could learn everything I need from you in just 45 minutes, but I could spend some time asking you some key questions to see if the product is really appropriate." They may hum and haw, but don't give them too many choices. Rather than asking if they'd like to meet, continue immediately with two meeting options: "Do you see any reason we can't meet on Thursday at 3:00, or possibly next Tuesday at 10:00?"[8]

With your calendar looking pretty booked up, the prospect is already thinking that you're the most popular salesperson around, so he is much more likely to fit you in. And if he isn't available at the times you suggest, show your magnanimity by rifling through your calendar and finding another slot, whether your calendar is full or not. "Let's see. I could end this meeting ten minutes early, and give you 40 minutes on Friday. Is that better for you?" By now you're not only a desired commodity. You are kind enough to share your time with him, and he'll appreciate you for that.

Next!

You may have the perfect Wow! statement. Your shiny toy may have awed your prospect. You may

> "*I think all great innovations are built on rejections.*"
> —Louis Ferdinand Celine

have knocked *No!* right out of the way and obtained permission to pursue. Even with your survey done, your prospect could still say, "Get out of my store! I have no interest in working with you! Go away! You're bothering me!"

That's right. We all get rejected, including all the best salesmen I know. It may be that you really have nothing that the client needs right

---

8   This is a classic example of the Alternative Choice close, which will be covered in "Chapter 8: Openings: The Chapter You Won't Need."

now, or they may want to wait a while before they tackle some particular problem. It may even be something stupid, like they don't like your tie. Regardless of what the reason is, if you feel in your gut that this prospect won't turn into a customer in the very near future, you're most likely right. So, don't be afraid to say "Thank you very much! I plan to keep working on winning your business and confidence, but I right now I don't think I have anything for you." Don't be afraid to say "Next!"

And don't take it as a loss either. When I get rejected, I like to think of the legendary Vince Lombardi, coach of the Green Bay Packers, who boasted how his team "never lost a game. They just ran out of time." Isn't time a precious commodity? That's why I'm never afraid to say "Next!" There are too many other prospects out there, and remember, prospecting is a numbers game!

To Add It All Up

Sales is just a big numbers game, so the way to win is to get those numbers up! In the next few chapters we'll look at ways to improve your ratios: if right now only ten out of twenty people are giving you the right time of day, we will look at ways to raise that ten to thirteen. If only five of those thirteen actually set up an appointment, we'll work on ways to get that five up to seven. If only three of those seven are worthy of hearing your pitch, our goal is to get that number to five. And of course, our goal is to close with at least three out of five, instead of a measly one.

But prospecting is another important way to get your numbers up. Think of it as a feeding machine, always supplying fresh meat to your ravenous appetite for closes. I mentioned earlier that at the Blinder Group I advise our clients that their sales reps target no less than twenty potential new prospects a week.

By now you should also realize that prospecting consists of four distinct steps, which follow one after the other in quick succession. Remember that whenever you're prospecting, you want to appear as busy as possible when you actually approach.

- Start the prospecting process with your **elevator statement**, delivered in a busy posture. Don't be afraid to look at your watch, and then jump right in to a concise but powerful statement about who you are and how the service you provide can help them grow their business with very little pain: "Benefit, benefit, benefit … and no pain!" This should take no more than 30 seconds!

- Follow that up immediately with your **shiny new toy statement**, explaining that the reason for interrupting them during their busy day is that you have a brand new product or service which you though would be a good match for their type of business. And if you don't have one, then make one up! All of this should take no more than 15 seconds.

- Get your prospect's **permission to pursue**. By now he knows that you're a salesperson, so get his permission to continue with the survey process. You can get this done in less than 10 seconds, meaning that the entire prospecting process is still well under a minute!

- Conduct a quick **survey** to make sure that this person really is the decision-maker you're looking for and to learn the names of all the other people who will influence the decision. There are plenty of people out there who can say no, but it is rare indeed to find someone who can say yes. Make sure you're meeting with the person or group of people who can say yes.

Prospecting is hard work – I believe that, emotionally, it is the hardest work that most salespeople do. There's nothing easy about facing rejection, and as much as we like to think we're Teflon, being told "No!" always hurts.

Now get out there and start prospecting!

Chapter II

Establishing Rapport

They don't care how much you know until they know how much you care.

—Zig Ziglar

The biggest mistake we make in sales is that we all love to talk. Let's face it. How many of us have thought that the more we sing the praises of our product, the more likely the prospect is to buy it? But that's all old school! Even in the best economy, the prospect knows whether he wants to buy or not within just 90 seconds of when you first walk through the door, and it doesn't matter if you're a new recruit or a sales-scarred veteran.[1] In a survival sales mode, the opening salvo is everything.

Of course, this doesn't mean that you should use that 90 seconds for rapid-fire staccato patter about yourself or your product. Stake out your position by building *rapport* and winning your client's trust. In sales, rapport is everything, or rather, almost everything. If there's one thing rapport is not, it's words. Back in 1969, Professor Albert Mehrabian of UCLA showed that feelings and attitude are expressed with 55 percent body language, 38 percent tone of voice, and just 7 percent words.[2] He called them "the three V's: Verbal, Vocal, Visual," but if you take a closer look you'll see how little weight the first V (Verbal) really has. It's a mistake to focus on that 7 percent at the expense of the other 93 percent.

---

1   See Larry Silvey. "The first 90 seconds," in *Aftermarket Business,* January 1, 2002.
2   Albert Mehrabian (1971). *Silent Messages.* Wadsworth Publishing Co.: Belmont, CA.

Our Clients, Our Friends?

It's too common for salespeople to think that their clients should be their friends. Have you ever heard the expression, "They buy

> *"I'm not concerned with your liking or disliking me ... All I ask is that you respect me as a human being."*
> — Jackie Robinson

you because they like you"? Well, forget it! Nothing is further from the truth, especially in a down economy. Perhaps in the '60s "relationship selling" worked, but these are challenging times we live in, and everyone – you and your prospects – is starting to feel the heat. Your prospects will certainly be grateful if you to treat them to dinner, a show, or a basketball game, but since these are troubling times, they've come to expect that from salespeople. It doesn't mean that they'll be more inclined to pass their hard-earned money to you. What they really want to know is that you're the kind of person who will work as hard as you can to help them meet their business goals. They'll respect you for that, and you want to win their respect.

Most of us know salespeople who go out for three-hour lunches with their clients, but barely manage to talk about those same clients' needs? They may write lunch off as a business expense, but did they get any business done? So don't share golfing stories – unless your prospect is selling golf clubs. You're not there to talk about their favorite restaurant; you're there to talk about their business and how the product you offer can help them *grow* it.

Before I go into a meeting, I ask myself how I want to be perceived. I have dear friends who I cherish, and customers who I appreciate. How do I want them to perceive me? The answer is usually as a business professional, who wants to help them grow their business.

So, should you meet with your clients? Yes! Should you earn their trust? Absolutely! But it's not about building a friendship with them. It's about establishing *rapport*, and good rapport will lead to great sales. So save your stories for your friends (no matter how pithy and funny those stories may be). When the call is all about them and very little about you, you are much closer to having the kind of relationship that you need to succeed.

Remember Their Names

One night, the concierge of my hotel arranged a wonderful evening for my wife and me at a little Italian

> *"The beginning of wisdom is to call things by their right names."*
> — Chinese proverb

bistro. He arranged for a car to take us there, and had the *maitre d'* reserve one of the best tables for us. He even instructed the restaurant to call the bell stand the moment we started our dessert, so that (without me knowing it) he could have a car waiting at the door when we were ready to leave: on the seat of the car there was a flower for my wife.

But that was not the best part of the evening. When we got back to the hotel, the doorman was waiting for us. He opened our car door and said, "Good evening, Mr. Blinder. Welcome home." You see, even if the concierge had gone home for the night, there was still a system in place to make sure that I got this personalized attention. I knew that they arranged dozens of cars for their guests every day, but when I heard him say my name, for one brief moment I felt that I was more than just a guest. The hotel and I had established rapport.

There is nothing more personal than a name, so learn your customer's name, repeat your customer's name, and use it every chance you get! People love to hear their names – don't you? – and using their names shows that you care about them as individuals – not just as some corporate figure that may or may not toss some money your way.

There are plenty of books with mnemonic devices to help you remember dozens of names at a glance. It's really that important in sales, and everywhere else in life. To me though, the easiest way to remember a name is to actually use it, again and again and again.

Chapter 2

Whenever I meet someone new, I repeat their name three times out loud. Now this may sound corny, but with a bit of practice you can easily work it into the conversation. For example, let's say you are meeting with Bill Curtis, Senior Vice President of Marketing for Omega Industries. "Bill!" you say, "Bill Curtis! How are you, Bill?" That's seven words and three Bills. If only all sales were as easy as that!

Sometimes, you can even personalize the dialogue. Rebekah Willliams is the Manager of an up-and-coming restaurant downtown. "Hello, Rebekah! Is that Rebecca with a *c* or Rebekah with a *k*?" You may already know the answer, but this shows her that you care, and it will help to drill the name into your head. When it comes to doing business, you're already one step ahead.

So what did you say your name is?

A Lean, Mean Sales Machine

Nobody has a perfect memory. There are always things we tend to forget, or

> *"He listens well who takes notes."*
> — Dante Alighieri

all those little hints that go unnoticed at first, until we take the time to reflect on them. After a long day of meetings with six or seven clients, will you really remember who wanted the ad copy for approval this Wednesdays or this Friday, or was interested in a run of site advertising inventory vs. targeted ads on the home page, even though the price may have scared them at first.

That's why at meetings I'll always ask permission to take notes. By taking notes I show that I'm listening; by asking permission to take notes I am giving the prospect a sense of empowerment and making him feel that his every word counts – that I am just there to carry out his instructions to the very last letter. Giving the prospect that sense of power is the very essence of rapport in sales, regardless of whether I actually jot down his every word, or make a list of the ingredients I need to pick up for dinner on my way home.

Of course it helps if you can use your notes to reconstruct your conversation with the prospect. Especially in tough economic times when you're out there competing for customers, you want to make sure that you have an edge which your competitors don't. You need to look better and act better to win each customer's trust. By taking notes you not only lend credence to the person you're meeting with; you signal to him that what he says really is important to you. And best of all, you have the information you need to remember whatever the heck he said.

My pad or notebook is an essential tool of my trade, and I take it with me to all my meetings. What I won't take with me when I first meet a new prospect is an overstuffed briefcase or a laptop. Now this may sound very old school at first, but I learned long ago that when I visit a new prospect toting a bulging briefcase, he immediately goes on the defensive and starts to worry about what I'm about to whip out. That's no way to build rapport. As for laptops, it's not that I'm a helpless Luddite: I love the latest gadgets as much as the next guy. But think of the last time you went to friends for dinner, and were greeted by a shiny projector in the living room. Do you really want to sit through 500 slides of their latest vacation in Hawaii or their daughter's school play? Does your prospect really want to sit through an interminable slide show about how great your product or service is? They could well be worried that the long presentation is hiding in your briefcase, just waiting to pop out at them. On the other hand, arriving unencumbered creates less initial stress and establishes much better rapport, especially with a new prospect!

My company is responsible for the sale of over $400 million dollars of very innovative interactive advertising products in client markets all over the world ... *without* the use of computers for most of the sales calls made. You should see the faces of the geeky website managers at the media companies we work with when we first explain that we can sell more of their products without us even cracking open a computer. But together, the sales training professionals who currently work for me make over 5,000 sales training calls a year using nothing more than 5-10 pages of printed sales presentations that briefly outline the features and benefits of the products we offer. Despite that, we still close long-term contracts with over 50 percent of our prospects in the initial sales call – and usually within 30 minutes of when we first meet the customer. No computer opened up with a PowerPoint™ presentation ready to go; no story boards popped out of a big, bulging briefcase.

That's why my greatest weapon is a simple leather folder that my wife got me for my birthday eleven years ago. To tell you the truth, even when I am in a meeting with a prospect I wait a while before I open the folder up. I'll establish eye contact, begin asking questions, and only then, after asking permission, will I begin to jot down my notes. The customer will not only appreciate the respect, but he will feel that what he's saying is important. By doing that, I'm winning his trust and establishing rapport.

Body Language

Do you remember the study by Professor Mehrabian that I mentioned at the start

> *"I speak two languages: Body and English."*
> — Mae West

of this chapter? He showed that 55 percent of feelings and attitude are expressed by body language. That's why face-to-face meetings are so important to establishing rapport with your prospects. Sadly, it sometimes feels as if this is a dying art.

I know that with the Internet, companies are having tremendous success using sales processes that do not require face-to-face meetings. Let's face it, Google™ is making billions of dollars by having their customers come to them and order their services on their own. I know that with rising gas prices, many companies don't want their salespeople to travel as much by car or by plane. Nevertheless, I also know that whenever I worked with sales organizations that try to cut back on face-to-face methods I've seen a downturn in actual closes. That's why I invest twice what is needed for web-training programs that I implement, which actually show my face on screen. When it comes to getting my point across, body language is everything.

Nonverbal communication is the perfect way for you to **soften** what you have to say:

S Smile
O Open posture
F Forward lean
T Touch
E Eye contact
N Nod

There's no replacement for the rapport that's established through the use of body language. In a fax or email, you can only get across 7 percent of what you want to say, and pick up 7 percent of what your prospect is telling you. You're missing 93 percent of the message! Phone calls may be better, because you can pick up on tone, and share 45 percent of what's really being said. It's only in face-to-face meetings, however, that you can get the whole package, by seeing when you get your point across – when your prospect's eyes light up and a smile crosses his face.

And your customer can see who they're dealing with too. They will pick up on the points that you want to emphasize through the cues you give them, no less than through the language you use. Sociologists actually distinguish between two types of non-verbal cues: *afferent cues*, which are cues that we receive, and *efferent cues*, which are cues that we send. It's important to know how to read our customers' afferent cues – for instance, a customer listening with arms folded across his chest is said to be in a defensive mode, which is obviously important to realize when you are making your pitch. In contrast, speaking to a customer with your palms held facing downward and moving up and down, actually makes what you're saying more convincing.[3]

Don't just take my word for it though. Watch political figures flailing their hands about on television—Nixon and Clinton were experts at this—or preachers pounding the pulpit in church. They're using their hands to sell their message, and you should be doing that too! Share the energy and excitement with your client! Just be careful not to dominate the dialogue.

Here's a fun experiment that you can do at parties. Look around the room until you find a group of people that obviously knows and likes each other. Notice how they all seem to adopt the same poses: if one leans against the wall, the others will also start leaning against the wall; if one of them puts down a cocktail, the others are sure to follow suit. Now you're ready to take the lead. The next time you're chatting with a small group of people, start nodding in agreement with the person talking, and see how long it takes before the others starting nodding along. Some people say, "Monkey see; monkey do." Psychologists call this *mirroring*. What it really means is using your whole body to listen and show empathy for what your partner is saying.

There are all sorts of ways you can mirror people to help establish rapport with them. Smile when they smile. Nod when they nod. You can adopt their posture and gestures, and you can imitate their tone of voice: excited or soft-spoken, quick or leisurely. Do they have any special catch phrases that you can incorporate into your conversation? Some outstanding "mirrorers" will even go so far as to try and breathe at the same pace as the person they are talking to.

One thing to be careful about though is that if you mirror your

---

3   One of the best books about nonverbal cues is Julius Fast's *Body Language* (Pocket Books, 1988). In it he offers a comprehensive overview of the most common gestures and how we interpret them subconsciously. Especially interesting is the difference between how certain gestures are interpreted differently based on whether it is a man or a woman making them.

The SOFTEN approach is used in many disciplines besides sales, and especially in education, where it is an important element of nonverbal communication between teacher and student. Jerry Eisner is a master salesman who developed the technique for use in sales. For more information, see his *First Impression Selling at Trade Shows: Winning Techniques that Create Instant Rapport*, a PDF downloadable from Amazon.com.

prospect, it does *not* turn into some grotesque imitation. You should not start to scratch your nose every time your prospect does. In fact, you will want to introduce subtle changes and get your prospect to start mirroring you. When you mirrored him, you showed him that you're thinking on his wavelength, but to make the sale you want him thinking on yours.[4]

Physical Contact

France is *not* famous for its culture of tipping. It was therefore surprising when French sociologists discovered that waitresses who touched the forearms of their clients, however briefly, actually began to receive tips for their service. While the importance of touch in business relations has long been known in the United States, it was not expected to cross national boundaries.[5]

But that's not all! It wasn't just waitresses, but waiters too. In a second study the same researchers found that slightly touching a client's forearm while recommending an item from the menu actually increased the customer's compliance. In other words, customers were more likely to order what their waitress (or waiter) suggested when the servers touched their forearms lightly.[6]

People respond to touch (and may even leave a larger tip). Of course, that doesn't mean that you should put your arm around your prospect while chatting, or give them a bear hug when coming or going. But occasionally, when appropriate, a gentle touch on the forearm may build just the right rapport, and help you clinch that deal!

---

4   Mirroring is part of a much larger field of nonverbal communications called neuro-linguistic programming (NLP). For a quick and easy overview of this exciting new field and how it can help you build rapport, see Romilla Ready and Kate Burton (2004). *Neuro-linguistic Programming for Dummies.* Wily Publishing, Inc.: Indianapolis, IN.
5   Nicolas Guégen and Céline Jacob (2004). "The effect of touch on tipping: an evaluation in a French bar," in *International Journal of Hospitality Management*, vol. 24, issue 2, June 2005, pp. 295–299.
6   Nicolas Guégen, Céline Jacob, and Gaëlle Boulbry (2007). "The effect of touch on compliance with a restaurant's employee suggestion," in *International Journal of Hospitality Management*, vol. 26, issue 4, December 2007, pp. 1019–1023.

To Tell the Truth

How can you tell when someone wants something from you? It's usually when they agree with just about everything you say. This is the

> *"To be persuasive, we must be believable; to be believable we must be credible; to be credible we must be truthful."*
> — Edward R. Murrow

kind of person who hears you like the Chicago Bulls, and is eager to tell you that they're his favorite team. "Who's your favorite player," you ask. "Oh, what's his name, the tall one," he'll inevitably answer, or "I'm not into individual players, but the team as a whole." You know right away that he knows nothing about the team (or the book, or the actor, or the wine), and you'll be skeptical of any of his future comments. He may have tried to build rapport, but by telling a white lie he actually ruined it. If trustworthiness is the most powerful weapon in the salesperson's arsenal, he was just disarmed by his little white lie, and you can bet he won't be making the sale.

But even if he makes the sale, was it really worth it? You can be assured that the customer remembers each and every little white lie. That salesperson may have closed the deal for now, but I have no doubt that when a more trustworthy competitor pops up, he will get the business.

So, when a prospect asks if you like fishing, don't say yes if what you really mean is picking interesting items off the menu at your local sushi bar. He means a rowboat on a lake at 4:00 am, and he'll know soon enough if you mean that too.

Of course, you don't have to annoy him by telling him how much the thought of that disturbs you. Be gently honest about your feelings, then find a way to identify with him, both then and in the future.

In fact, I'm sometimes asked about fishing, a pastime that I never had the time to explore. But I'll still try to find a way to connect, identifying with my prospect's passion but not hiding the fact that I don't share it. "You know, I never really found the time to fish, which is odd because my parents loved it. Every summer they would go to this little place in Virginia and come back with a boatload of flounder." He knows that I am not a fisherman, but he also knows that I can empathize with his fondness for the sport. Most of all, he knows that I am credible, and that makes me all the more persuasive.

Listening

Let's face it! Telemarketers can sometimes be annoying. But every so often they have

> *"One must talk little and listen much."*
> — African proverb

just the product you've been looking for. It happened to me a while ago. A telemarketer was trying to sell me something that I really wanted. Inevitably, I had lots of questions, but the poor guy had a script, and he insisted on sticking to it. Rather than simply taking my business, he was actually ignoring me so that he could get my business. *Ignoring* me so that he could get my business! He didn't because I took that as rude.

We can talk about names and business cards, about body language and physical contact, but if you really want to build rapport with your prospects and convert them into business partners, the most important thing you must do is listen. What do they want? What do they need? How can you help them? Only after you really understand this can you offer them the perfect solution, and *really understanding* means *really listening*. There's a reason the oldest adage in sales is, "He who speaks loses."

Listening to your client is more than just a form of silent flattery. It is also an important strategic tool in your sales arsenal. The African proverb above says that "One must talk little and listen much." This could be because we think at least five times faster than we speak, so listening gives us the advantage of planning ahead and developing strategy while the customer is talking. In contrast, if the customer is listening to you wax poetic about your product, he has plenty of time to think of ways to get rid of you.

It takes a lot practice to listen offensively (rather than defensively). Use body language to show that you are listening, and echo your customer's thoughts by repeating key words and phrases. If he says, "We're having problems drawing a crowd on Wednesday," nod your head and repeat "Wednesday?" This not only shows that you understand what he is saying, but that you empathize with his needs. Even more importantly, it may encourage him to continue with his next thought, and reveal even more about those needs. This technique, called "echoing," keeps your prospect talking and you in control.

And you are in control of the dialogue. When you select the keywords and probe the key ideas, the prospect is more likely to elaborate on them: "Yes, Wednesday, because we're closed on Monday, and Tuesday is our 'Buy one, get one free' night."

Most importantly, only speak when absolutely necessary. I've been on hundreds of "four-legged sales training calls," accompanying media sales reps, and only regret that I didn't have a dime for all the times I needed a cattle prod to stun the person with me into silence. He who speaks loses! He who speaks loses! He who speaks loses! It's the most important lesson in this chapter, if not in this entire book.

Why? Because too many people like to ramble, so avoid it at all costs. Know in advance exactly what you want to say, and how long it will take you to say it. In his book *60 Seconds & You're Hired!*,[7] Robin Ryan suggests actually giving yourself a time limit of no more than one minute for an overview of your most important points, then have your customer tell you how much detail he wants about those specific points. Once again, time your responses, so that they last no more than a minute. Your customer will appreciate this, and it will give you a chance to understand his needs better.

Even the smoothest talkers will benefit from remembering what Supreme Court Justice John Marshall once said: "To listen well is as powerful a means of communication *and influence* as to talk well"

7   Robin Ryan, *60 Seconds & You're Hired!*, Penguin, 2008.

(the italics are my own). Economist Bernard Baruch took it one step further, saying "Most of the successful people I've known are the ones who do more listening than talking." To influence and succeed! Isn't that what sales are all about?

But What About Me?

Now let's take it one step further too. If you should be listening, not talking, it would seem pretty obvious that you shouldn't be talking about

> *"People are self-centered*
> *To a nauseous degree;*
> *They keep talking about themselves,*
> *When it's all about me!"*
> — Piet Hein

yourself. Unfortunately, some people don't think so. In fact, there are too many salespeople who try to win sympathy for themselves to close deals.

Have you ever asked, "How are you?" and gotten an actual response? "Well, I just had an enormous fight with my wife, and it looks like my car needs a new engine. Meanwhile, my son is failing math, my daughter is dating some kid I don't approve of, the dog is sick, the roof is leaking, my blood pressure is soaring, and the baby is teething. Other than that, I'm okay."

You may as well hear it from me first: Nobody cares, least of all your prospect. He has his own list of problems, most of them centered on his business, and as we'll see in the next chapter, you're there to solve them. So keep all of your problems at home, and focus exclusively on his.

A few years ago I managed to get a meeting with the *Tampa Tribune*, a very important media company just an hour from my home. I was about to meet with sixteen top executives to pitch my company's approach to sales. Everything seemed to be going my way.

But a few days earlier my uncle tried to sell me one of his used vintage sports cars. It was an absolutely beautiful vehicle, and I was a sucker for his "Puppy Dog close" (more on that in Chapter 8): "Why don't you take it home and try it? That way you can see if you like it." So two hours before the meeting – I always like to get there early – I got into the car and headed off to Tampa.

It was one of the smoothest rides I ever had, until somewhere along the way the brakes gave in. There I was, heading to one of the most important meetings of the year, in a vintage sports car without any brakes. When I left I wasn't sure if I would get their business; now I wasn't sure if I would get there alive.

Somehow I managed to get off the highway and come to a stop in a car dealer's lot. I ran inside to explain my predicament, and promised that the car would be towed, but only after I made it to the meeting. Then I called a rental car service, which delivered a car right away to where I was. I may have broken the speed limit the rest of the way, but I got to that meeting with three minutes to spare.

"How are you, Mike?" my contact greeted me.

"Just great," I answered, and we got down to business. After the meeting, I called my wife and told her about everything that had happened. The only people who never found out were the executives at the *Trib*, and the reason for that is simple. I was there to solve their problems, *not* to share my problems with them. I made them feel that they were my priority, and that's what rapport is all about.[8]

---

8   When I tell this story at the lectures I give, the first question I'm usually asked is whether I got their business. I did, but I usually add that I'm not sure I would have if, instead of focusing on their needs, I'd spent that meeting talking about the problems I had getting there.

Chapter III

The ABC of Diagnosis

Asking questions is the ABC of diagnosis. Only the inquiring mind solves problems.

—Edward Hodnett

Sales should be a dirty word. It implies that someone is only out to make money, when a good salesperson is there to help his customers. Let's face it. None of us lives in a perfect world, and we're all trying to make our lives easier. The real challenge is that we don't always know exactly what our problem is, or what it would take to make things better. The best we can do is to find someone to help us identify the challenge and come up with an appropriate solution. That's exactly what a good salesperson does.

So, once we've already established rapport and won our customer's trust, the next thing to do is to find out exactly how we can help.

That's right. Help. If you believe in your product – and every good salesperson should – you realize that what you are offering is the best solution for some problem that the prospect has. Is he trying to save money? Then you have a cost-effective solution for his printing or delivery needs. Is she spending too much time traveling to meet customers? Then you might have the perfect web-based meeting system for her. Are they upset that their restaurant is empty on Tuesdays? Then hopefully your ad campaign will pack the house. The idea is to know precisely what the need is so that you can offer a tailor-made solution. But before showing off your products, you have to ascertain your prospect's needs.

Chapter 3

Have I Got a Deal for You!

Don't you love it when you walk into a meeting, and before you even begin your pitch – before you

> *"If the only tool you have is a hammer, you tend to see every problem as a nail."*
> — Abraham Maslow

even polish your rapport – the customer greets you with a smile and a question: "What have you got for me today?"

Hurray! You passed the finish line and you didn't even have to open your mouth. He knows you're there to sell him something, and he just wants to see what it is. I guess you owe him that much, don't you? So put down this book, whip out your latest product, and sell it fast and furiously!

Sure, that's one approach to sales, but it's definitely not my approach. So with your permission, I'd like to start this section again.

Have I Got a Deal for You! (Take 2)

Don't you hate it when you walk into a meeting, and before you even begin your pitch – before you even polish your rapport – the customer greets you with a smile and a question: What have you got for me today?

Ouch! You know your customer isn't really interested. This meeting is more of a courtesy for him, or in some cases just a formality. He's bought the same thing again and again, regardless of whether it's an ad in the Yellow Pages or some toner for the copy machine. It's a tradition, not business, and you're far from getting at the crux of what sales are: ways that you can help your customers. If only you could read the mind of a customer when he says, "What have you got for me today?" If you could, you'd hear him say in no uncertain terms: "Speak fast and get out!"

That's one reason why master salespeople always warn against getting into the rut of buying and selling the exact same thing year after year, with only the price tag adjusted for inflation. Yet too many people continue to do this. It may be because this is an easy way to keep their numbers up, or perhaps they do it because they don't have the courage to shake up what seems like a "good thing." Instead they take what I like to call a "Chinese restaurant" approach to sales – a neat little menu with items and prices – and let the customer decide.

This must stop!

And it will. In a down economy, when the herd is being culled, these people are peddlers, not salespeople, and peddlers are always the first casualties!

The survivors are salespeople who use "solution-based selling," or the "consultative approach," as it is sometimes known. They're finding out exactly what their customers' needs are and tailoring solutions to meet every possible problem. I take it as a rule of thumb that what worked last year won't work this year. The world is changing way too fast for that, and so are your customers' needs. So find out what their current needs really are – and by current I mean this month or this week – before you make your pitch.

This is certainly true in my industry, newspaper advertising, where everything is changing quickly. Classified ads were once a revenue staple, but today they're forced to compete with Craig's List™ and countless other websites. But it's also true of so many other products, whether it's new cars and airlines competing against rising gas prices, or telephone service providers competing against Broadband. Each of these presents a whole new set of problems for you to identify and solve. So remember, you're selling solutions, not products.

Absolutely Nothing

A few years ago, I had a meeting in New York with the head of one of the biggest businesses that

> *"To do nothing at all is the most difficult thing in the world, the most difficult and the most intellectual."*
>
> — Oscar Wilde

specializes in internet advertising. To prepare for this meeting I did all my homework: I crossed all my *t*'s and dotted all my *i*'s. My PowerPoint™ presentation was sparkling. I was ready to shine! When this prominent businessman walked into the conference room surrounded by his entourage, he looked me straight in the eye and asked, "What have you got for me today?" Instead of handing him my presentation, I looked at him and said, without skipping a beat, "Absolutely nothing!"

For one split second, you could hear the tension. I'd been waiting months for a chance to meet this leader of a booming industry, and just about everyone thought I was wasting his time. But I jumped right in: "I want to hear what you need first, before I start offering solutions." His staff may have been in shock, but he understood exactly what I meant. We were talking salesman to salesman, so he got out of his chair, walked over, and hugged me. Then, turning to his team he said: "This is someone I can do business with." And we've been doing business ever since. He realized that I could have made my pitch and tried to sell him something that he didn't need, like dozens of other salespeople before me. But instead, to make the meeting worthwhile, I first chose to know exactly what he needed. Without that, there was nothing I could sell him. I was there to solve a problem, not to sell a product, and before I began to solve that problem, I had to know what the problem was. Fortunately, he appreciated that, but that's probably why his business is thriving.

The Most Common Mistake

Not every salesperson realizes that the job is really problem-solving, and not just acting as a middleman (which is more or less what *entrepreneur* means). How many times have you gone into a clothing store to try on a jacket or a dress? In most cases, the routine is the same. You find a jacket you like on the rack, and an eager salesperson comes up and asks: "Can I help you?" I'm willing to bet your answer is always, "No, thank you. I was just browsing."

But let's imagine another scenario. A woman is in the same store looking at a green cocktail dress. A saleswoman, spotting her as a potential new customer, walks over to her and says, "I may be able to save you some time. Are you just looking for this style, because we have a larger selection of cocktail dresses over there?"

Now the customer is befuddled. It's easy to brush off the old "Can I help you?" but what can she possibly say now? She can't answer, "No, I was only browsing," so she fumbles for the next best thing: "I do like this one, but I think I would prefer it in black."

Our intrepid saleswoman doesn't miss a beat. "Black? Yes, that would look great on you! I think we have one over here. What kind of neckline are you looking for?" And with the dress on one arm and the customer on the other, she leads her to an adjacent rack with the same dress in black. By now, the saleswoman has taken control of the situation, and is ready to make the close. "What length are you looking for?" What else can the customer possibly ask for, except, perhaps, some matching accessories?

What this saleswoman did – and what her colleague in men's wear failed to do – was ask probing questions to identify her customer's needs, and help her find the perfect solution. Rather than simply offering to help, she ascertained the problem and immediately came up with the right answer. In sales, the questions you ask are everything. You'll never ascertain your customer's needs until you start asking about what those needs are.

Ascertaining New Prospects

Whether you're facing a new prospect or an existing advertiser, the ascertainment process begins when you query your targets about their current goals, needs, and

> "… *the art of making problems so interesting and their solutions so constructive that everyone wants to get to work and deal with them.*"
>
> — Paul Hawken

desires, and understand how they want to improve their business. When dealing with a new client, you should already know exactly what type of business it is and have some ideas about the kinds of products that might help them. Even before you speak to the owner of a restaurant, you should know whether the menu offers steak or Chinese food, and have a rough idea about the clientele that it attracts. Is it competing with a burger joint or a Fodor's 4-fork establishment run by a celebrity chef? Once you know this, you can begin to assess the ways that you might be able to help them make their business grow.

But even with all the good intentions in the world, always remember that the customer isn't stupid. They know you want to sell them something, and you may even be the tenth person that day to call on them with a "miracle product." As soon as you walk in the door, assume that they are on the defensive, and take back the initiative.

The German philosopher Arthur Schopenhauer observed that "It is … when he is off-guard that a man best reveals his character." You want to catch your prospect off-guard to understand what he really wants for his business, beyond clichéd answers like "To see it grow." This is survival selling at its best, because like Sun Tzu said, "Surprise will lead to victory."

And you do want to surprise your customers – especially your new prospects. If the best surprise is no surprise, then best surprise in sales is no product. It's often the case that when you start talking to them, they'll give the impression that everything is great and business is going as well as it could, so you couldn't possibly have something to offer them. It's a logical response too. After all, they are talking to someone they just met. They're not likely to share all their problems with you. As far as many of them are concerned, you're just another problem, or rather, just a nuisance.

But rest assured that every businessperson has something that keeps him up at night. It could be rising prices or steep competition. It could be a changing clientele, or perhaps a changing neighborhood. In the best scenarios they'll likely be surprised to find out how much you actually know.

So the rule of thumb for a successful first meeting is never, ever discuss your product! Don't even mention it! Discuss your customer's business instead. Surprising? Well, think about it. Would you trust a lawyer who told you to sue without knowing whether it was a car crash or a contractor? Would you trust a car salesman who tried to push a Ferrari on you, when you really need a van to get the kids to school? Would you trust a doctor who prescribed you medication without even asking what your symptoms are? As I always like to say, "Prognosis without diagnosis is malpractice!"

So use that first meeting to state your purpose. "I pass your store at least twice a week, and I just wanted to learn a little more about you and see if there's some way we might do business together." Does he know that you really want to sell him something? Absolutely! But frankly, he can't just come out and say "I don't want to do business with you" before he actually knows what you're offering. And most of all, what you've really done is express an interest in him and his work, and if there's one topic we're all happy to talk about, it's about ourselves and our work.

Effectively, you've just opened a door that will help you get to know this prospect's needs.

Ascertaining Current Customers

If I had a dime for all the sales reps I rode with, who said, "I didn't know that!" after we both met with their customers, I would have retired ten years ago and lived comfortably off the interest. It's shocking when I consider how many sales reps I work with who call on the same customers year after year but don't ask them any relevant new questions. In contrast, when I'm there, I'll immediately start probing: "Do you spend money on competing media?" or "Are you currently looking at other initiatives?" By simply asking whether they are undergoing changes – or even just considering changes – I will uncover enormous amounts of vital information that the current salesperson knew nothing about. Yet this is precisely the information they should be looking for if they've spent years maintaining a business relationship with that very customer!

Yes, it is surprising what you learn when you ask, which is why the ascertainment process should not be relegated to new prospects only. It must continue with existing customers. Even if you have a long-term contract, you should be out there on a regular basis, not just servicing existing needs, but uncovering new needs too. In fact, this is absolutely vital!

Vital? Yes it is, for two important reasons. By repeating the ascertainment process with your established customers at fairly regular intervals, you are likely to learn about their latest needs – the very same needs that you can address with your latest products, and thereby actually boost your sales, instead of just coasting along. But survival sales consists of playing offense and defense, and in this case defense is no less important. Have you really considered what your competitors are up to while you sit there quietly, taking advantage of a "sure thing"? The chances are that they're ogling your customers, and trying to figure out what they can do to swipe their business right out from under you! If you don't ascertain your customers' needs regularly, you'll never even know just how precarious your business relationships might be! You are far more likely to be caught off guard by that dreaded phone call: "Your order has been cancelled."

Complacency kills sales!

Know Their Pain

In the chapter on rapport we saw how important it is to keep people talking. Fortunately, people love to

> *"A question asked in the right way often points to its own answer."*
> — Edward Hodnett

talk, whether it's about their lives or businesses, so it's actually quite simple to ascertain their needs. With the right amount of empathy and some select questions funneled properly, they'll tell you just about everything you need to know.

It's very important to funnel your question, starting with the broadest, simplest topics. With a new prospect, you can start off with the most fundamental questions about their business: "How long have you been doing this? What got you into it? How do you handle potential competition?" Find out about their customers as well: "What is their income bracket? Do they show loyalty and return, or is it mostly a one-time deal?" With each answer, penetrate even deeper.

If you are ascertaining with an established customers, you should already know this basic information (unless, of course, there have been significant changes under the radar), so you can get right down to the nitty-gritty about the challenges they face today. There is actually no better time to do this than in a down economy. Take it as a rule of thumb that "When people have pain, you must ascertain!" and there's no greater pain than a down economy and a country on the verge of financial crisis.[1] "How has the banking crisis impacted you? How does it affect your future plans?" whether for the next month, the next quarter, or the next year. And while it may not be obvious to you, their competition is constantly changing too, so questions about their current business rivals are especially valuable when ascertaining the needs of established customers. Just keep delving, from the broadest, most general questions to the most specific. Imagine in advance what their needs might be, how urgent they are, and how they cope with them. Do their problems demand an immediate solution, or can they wait a few months? If the latter is the case, this won't help you hit your numbers next month, so keep

---

1   Between writing and reviewing this chapter, the Federal Government has approved the $700 billion rescue package for the country's leading financial institutions, the Dow Jones has plunged almost 1000 points in a single day, and the word *Recession* is on everyone's lips. No one knows how this will end, but according to most commentators the prognosis is dire. With holiday sales expected to hit an all-time slump, it's fair to say that B2B sales really has become a struggle to survive.

on probing until you find a more immediate problem that you can solve right then and there. Of course, you should make a note of the original problem for future reference, because you will be able to get billing from it sometime down the road.

If you find that your customer is reluctant to talk – and some businesspeople really are reluctant – asking the right question will usually hit a nerve and get them to open up to you.

I showed this to one of my client's sales reps when I accompanied him on a call to a cash-advance business. The rep was eager to get the business, but was constantly told, "Everything's going as well as can be. Just about everyone knows about us." Needless to say, I was skeptical. "We're sorry to have taken your time," I told the manager, "I guess you really don't need our help with advertising after all." With that the sales rep and I headed to the door. After all, what salesman wants to be annoying? But as we were about to leave, I spun around, just like Columbo,[2] and added: "One more thing: you know that we're just six minutes away, but on our ride over here I counted six other businesses doing the exact same thing you do." I immediately hit a raw nerve, and was subject to a long barrage of complaints about the competition and how this particular establishment was much more reliable, how its rates were better, and how those other places are cheating their clients. Did I say the barrage was long? Actually, it wasn't that long, because within twenty minutes we had clinched the deal and had their order for a six-month ad campaign!

With information about potential sore spots at your fingertips, you're already beginning to identify ways that you can help your prospect. Once the conversation progresses, you can begin to focus more on the specifics – the kinds of problems you want to solve. At first the information will trickle in slowly, but you'll soon be surprised at how quickly it becomes a flood. Your customers will appreciate that you haven't tried to sell them anything, so there's no reason for them to be on the defensive now.

---

2   More on this in Chapter 8, where I discuss the infamous "Columbo Close."

A Few Simple Steps

I've already hinted at a few simple steps you can use to get your prospects to open up. Here they are, in a nutshell:

- **Research:**

Once upon a time, a salesperson could spend hours in the magazine stacks of the local library to find out about a potential customer's business. Things are very different these days, thanks largely to the Internet, so take advantage of that amazing tool, and add it as a weapon in your growing arsenal. Find out about the prospect's branch of business and the kinds of problems similar businesses face, then ask your prospect how she handles those problems on a day-to-day basis. For instance, when I first entered sales, I began to sell radio advertising to restaurants. While researching the topic, I discovered that restaurants tend to do most of their business on Thursdays, Fridays, and Saturdays, while the rest of the week is comparatively slower. Eager to solve this problem, and possibly find more business for my advertisers, I raised the point during a meeting: "I took the liberty," I told a client, "of doing some research about your industry. One spokesperson said that this [*i.e.*, the drop in weekday business] is the case, and I was wondering if you found that to be true locally." Upon learning that Tuesdays were his weakest nights, I was able to win his business with a plan to develop and advertise a new "Tuesday night special." With a little research and a carefully planned question, I was able to identify a problem and come up with a precise solution for it. I looked more professional than any potential competitors because I came in armed with research. I looked more empathetic because I showed that I wanted to learn more about the growth of their business.

Since then, I've developed my own way of doing research, which I'm about to share with you. Use Google News! Just type in the generic term for the kind of business you're looking to sell to, followed by the word "industry." So, for example, if I wanted to sell advertising to a flower shop, I'd look up "florist industry" and learn that walk-in traffic is down sharply, that wedding costs are being cut because of hard times, and, of course, that the anticipated "July sag" is taking its toll in sales. If I type in "auto parts aftermarket industry," I'd learn about rising steel costs, and the problem with counterfeit parts. The best thing is that I'd learn all of that in less time than it would take me to drive to the library. In the case of these two industries, which I researched this past July, my computer time amounted to less than 3 minutes. In other words, I found an entire litany of problems to solve for two very distinct industries in under 180 seconds. Yet, with this information in hand, I have several important issues I can raise when conducting an ascertainment, regardless of whether it is with new prospects or established customers.

- **What do you mean by that?**

When information isn't forthcoming, get your customer to expand on what they're saying with six simple words: "What do you mean by that?" So if some restaurant owner tells you that anticipated revenues in the next quarter are expected to grow by 25 percent, follow up with "What do you mean by that?" You may get an answer like, "Traffic is growing by 40 percent, but we have to redo our interior and expand seating, which will mean a cut in our profits." Once again: "What do you mean by that?" Pretty soon she'll have identified her long-term plans, along with all the hurdles she faces along the way. As a salesperson it is now your job to help eliminate those hurdles.

- **Snap your fingers:**

In sales we do a special kind of magic to help resolve people's problems. One tried and true method, as old as sales itself, is to hint to your customers that you can do the kind of magic that they are probably looking for. "If I could snap my fingers and solve your problems, what would you like to see happen?" In other words, what kind of solutions are you looking for, given your current circumstances? While the question may sound corny, it really gets to the crux of the matter, and it leaves them open to another question, which is actually no less important for you: "What is it worth to you?" With this, you not only know about your customers' particular problems: you also have a better grip on the kind of budget they're willing to spend to solve them. You're honing in on their aspirations, and figuring out what your role will be in finding the right solution. And don't be embarrassed about asking this question either. You're there to talk business, and they recognize that. In fact, I've never had anyone who refused to answer, "What's it worth to you?" Every businessman realizes that magic comes with a price attached; every salesperson needs to know right away whether their prospects can really afford them.

- **What did you dislike about your previous sales reps?**

Face it! We all love to complain, and when given the chance we'll go on and on with a litany of problems and grievances. Prospects are no different, and when asked about their current or previous suppliers, they'll be sure to let you know about every single complaint they had. If they cost too much, you'll be sure to hear about it, and if delivery was always late, you'll get an earful about that too. More often than not, your prospect will fill you in on all the smallest details about the quality, the service, the price, the efficiency, and whatnot. So nod your head sympathetically and say, "Yes, yes, yes" Hear their pain! And while they are speaking take meticulous notes, so that by the end of the meeting you will know their objections before they actually raise them. You'll have in front of you a long list of everything your proposal should avoid. Just remember that you are ascertaining now, so bite your tongue and do absolutely nothing to address these issues at this time. Save that for the pitch!

- **How would you like your customers to refer to you?**

With all due respect to William Shakespeare, "that which we call a rose, by any other name would *not* smell as sweet," at least not in advertising. That's why, when I sell advertising, I ask the clients upfront how they want their customers to refer to them, especially their most satisfied customers. Do they want to be known as "the biggest," "the best," "the cheapest," "the fastest," "the most reliable," or the "most entertaining"? With this information, I'll have a grasp on their product's "unique selling proposition," and use this "USP" as the focus of my ad campaign.

Above all, it gives me an idea of how they want to be perceived, even if they are not perceived that way now – and if they are not perceived that way, what I can do to help them earn that reputation. That's why this question can actually be important even if you aren't selling advertising. All businesses want to be perceived a certain way. Once you know what that is, you can focus your pitch on helping them get there, regardless of what you're selling them.

Sun Tzu said "Know where your enemy is." While he's hardly an enemy, your prospect is the person you want to win over. With these five simple techniques, you know exactly "where he is." You've uncovered the roots of your prospect's pain, and have all the information you need to offer him a solution. You've identified the problem (*Research*), gone into depth about how it affects them (*What do you mean by that?*), learned how they would like to see it fixed and at what cost (*Snap your fingers*), discussed potential problems along the way (*What do you dislike about your sales reps?*) and found out how they want to be perceived (*How do you want your customers to refer to you?*).

You'll also want to listen closely for any potential objections that your customer may have. When you come back to make your pitch, especially if you use the two-call approach, that very same customer will have had the time to come up with all the best reasons why to turn you down and say no. If, however, you get a sense of what those potential objections might be, you will be able to hone your pitch to answer them before they are actually made! If, for example, you realize that the greatest objection you will face will be the cost, you can add an explanation of the price directly into your pitch, and deprive the objection of most of its steam.

So when you're ascertaining needs, try and ascertain potential objections too. With that, most of your work is done, and your customer actually did it for you.

Still No Product!

You did all that with out even mentioning once what it is you actually sell. That's because in survival sales, you're really selling solutions, not products. Since your prospect opened up to you, now it's time to show him how seriously you take everything he had to say.

By the end of the ascertainment process you should be able to answer the following questions:

- What is the problem that you plan on solving?

- How much is the customer willing to invest in finding a solution for this problem?

- When does your customer want to see this problem solved?

If you've done your job and delved deeply enough, there are a few additional pieces of information that you should also have:

- How motivated are your customers to actually solve this problem? Is it really a top priority, or do they have other, more pressing needs? While you may get their business by addressing one need, you may get more business by addressing another.

- What objections might they have to the proposal that you will eventually make? It's always best to preempt these with answers before you customer can actually object or, at least, to prep for the counter you will have to make to field that objection.

My company has made millions of dollars on single-meeting closes, but I learned sales with a two-meeting approach, which allows me to write a proposal, plan a solution, and even put together some speculative ideas to show my customer. So, after I'm done with the ascertainment process, even if I have great ideas buzzing around my head, my preferred approach is to disconnect, so that I can do more research and put together a winning proposal.

However, if you are planning a two-meeting approach, never disconnect before you have that second meeting marked firmly in your calendar. One good way to do this is to turn to your customer and say: "I've heard some really great things here, and I think I can assist you. I'd like to go back and work with our team to put together some solid ideas. I assume you'll want to hear about them."

Permit me, however, one word of caution. Don't be surprised if the next time you meet with your customer some of the magic of that first meeting is gone. He may even act antagonistically. The fact that you're coming back tells him right away that he caved, and that he let you charge right though the main gate. He shared his weakness and told you what it would take to overcome it. Now you're coming back with that very solution. He knows that you are well on your way to selling him what he needs. He is back on the defensive, which is why salespeople must resolve their great dilemma: do they go straight for the close or retreat? Do they have one meeting or two?

Chapter IV

The Great Dilemma:
One Meeting or Two?

Don't be afraid to take a big step if one is indicated; you can't cross a chasm in two small steps.

—David Lloyd George

Perhaps the biggest question I face every time I meet with a new client is whether to "go right for the kill," or to hold it off for a second meeting. My gut instinct tells me to close – that's what salesmen are there for. But then again, I can't help thinking of Sun Tzu, who warned against the speedy attack, even if you think you are ready. "The good fighters of old first put themselves beyond the possibility of defeat, and then waited for an opportunity to defeat the enemy."

Am I really beyond all possibility of defeat? Have I covered all my bases? Have I researched my client's needs and come up with the best possible solution? On the other hand, the guy loves me now! If I don't go right in for the close I'll have to start building all this rapport again, and by then he may realize I'm coming to sell him something. And what if one of my competitors corners him and closes in the meantime?

What do I do? Do I disconnect or close? Didn't Vince McMahon say that "Sometimes you have to take a half step back to take two steps forward"?

What do you do?

A Dilemma to Deal With

A dilemma is really just a coin toss. We're faced with two options that are equally good, or alternately, that are equally

> *"Our dilemma is that we hate change and love it at the same time; what we really want is for things to remain the same but get better."*
> — Sydney Harris

bad. When dealing with one meeting or two, the biggest problem we face is that we don't actually have the time to pull out a pad and start putting together a personalized proposal that addresses the customer's needs. We have to charge forward with what we have right now, using the momentum from coming down the first slope to get us to the top of the second. It is a lot like riding a bicycle. You've just glided down one hill, and you may be able to use that built up energy to get you right to the top of the next.

But Sir Edmund Hillary used to say that "It's not the mountain we conquer but ourselves." If sales is more like mountain climbing than cycling, perhaps we do need to set up a base camp and prepare ourselves, both mentally and physically, for the final assault. In most cases that second slope will always be there, daunting us and demanding that we conquer it. So ask yourself if you have what you need to make sure you get yourself over the second slope – in terms of equipment no less than of energy – or whether you wouldn't be better off returning to base camp and preparing yourself for it.

Regardless of what you eventually decided – and each case should be judged individually – this much should be obvious by now. There are always two steps to sales: you can't pitch before you ascertain, and you really shouldn't waste time ascertaining if you don't intend to pitch. The real question is whether you gear up in the valley, because once you've reach the top of that second slope, it's an easy ride down to the pot of gold at the bottom.

If the world of sales ever decided that it needed a mascot, it would probably pick the Bactrian camel.* Its two humps — the first smaller than the second — are a perfect metaphor for the two slopes that every salesperson needs to overcome in order to reach the close. The first hump is the ability to get in the door, see the decision-maker, build rapport, and do an ascertainment. The second hump is the ability to deliver the pitch and close.

Always Keep in Mind

Now that you know both sides of the coin, there is another important thing to remember. It won't always be your decision. That's right. As thrilled as your prospective new customer may be by everything you've been telling him, he is a businessperson just like you, with a very busy schedule. If you were slotted to meet for an hour, and you only have fifteen minutes left, is that enough time to address his objections and give the pitch the kind of attention it deserves? Or will it be a rushed pitch, with interruptions and less of a chance to field some genuine questions? This is where we get back to body language.

---

*   This is a public domain image by Bbullot. The original can be found at http://commons.wikime-dia.org/wiki/Image:Bactrian_camel.jpg. The copyright holder of this image allows anyone to use it for any purpose, including unrestricted redistribution, commercial use, and modification.

Looking for Signals

When deciding whether to proceed or disconnect, you must read your customer's body language carefully. Is he always checking his watch or shuffling papers on his desk? Is her secretary always popping in to say that so-and-so called "urgently"? In that case it is probably worthwhile to wait, and come back with a comprehensive proposal, i.e., one that the customer will pay more attention to.

Or alternately – and this happens too – is your prospect so excited about your product that he tells his secretary to clear the next half hour so that he can continue talking to you. Is he starting to talk about the features of your product as if they were benefits to his business? Then you know that you're getting what we call, "buying signals." And if the signals are right, it's time to move forward.

I've always believed that "The opposite of love is not hate, but indifference."[1] So if your customer is responding with indifference, you know the time has come for you to schedule a follow-up meeting and disconnect. But if you begin to hear sincere questions about what you're presenting, you can rest assured that the customer is excited and eager to move forward. Questions mean interest, and interest is one of the foremost buying signals.

But there are other signals too. When the customer turns your features into benefits, you know that she is already interested. And when he begins talking about the product as if he already owns it, you should probably jump right in and deliver your pitch. Listen carefully for "post-agreement" questions too, such as "How do you do the billing cycle?" or "How do I know when these ads run?" or "Will I get copies to review with my partners?" These are all important buying signals. Finally, never feel intimidated if the customer begins to haggle about the price, because that is a major buying signal too.

The trick is to be able to gauge buying signals and not to misinterpret them based on your own eagerness to sell. Beware of what Mark

---

1   Elie Wiesel.

Dembo calls "driving down a road of false hope toward the land of 'Pendingville.'"[2] While you must always take notice of your customer's buying signals, you have to be able to distinguish them from the "not-buying signals," and even from the "not-buying-right-now signals." But, if the buying signals are indisputable, if your customer starts talking about your product as if it's already his, well, as my first mentor in sales always said: "Don't leave any meat on the table!"

The Perfect Solution

Then what's the dilemma? The answer is simple. There are times when you just aren't ready yet, no matter how eager your prospect may be. Ask yourself honestly, not only if you can get to the close, but whether the close that you can get to is ideal. You may be able to sell something now, but if you wait and prepare for the next meeting, you may be able to make a better pitch and get twice the amount of business.

Zig Ziglar is a master salesman whose approach I've often adopted in my own sales. If I had to sum up one lesson I've learned from him, it is "Sell by design, not by chance." In fact it is the title of a chapter in his book *Selling 101.*[3] So, even if you feel really confident that you can make the close immediately, ask yourself honestly whether you are selling by design, or if you just happened to hit pay dirt on the day your prospect just happens to be in a good mood. No one should ever turn down a winning ticket, but playing the lottery is never a good business strategy either.

Rebuilding Rapport

One of the biggest challenges we face in sales is building rapport with our clients. But the truth is that in your first meeting, it is not as difficult as you may imagine. Do you remember how I told you that you must never actually mention your product when you are establishing rapport

---

2   See "Buying Signals: Is Your Prospect Really Ready to Buy?" on *The Sideroad: Practical Advice Straight from the Experts* (http://www.sideroad.com/Sales/buying-signals.html).

3   Zig Zilgar. *Selling 101*, The Zig Ziglar Corporation, 2003.

or conducting an ascertainment? It makes the prospect all the more relaxed, and the meeting so much less threatening. Your prospect likes you precisely because you haven't tried to sell him anything. In fact, if he did most of the talking, he hasn't really put much thought into why you were even there in the first place.

But when deciding whether to go right into the pitch or to wait for a second meeting, the question to ask is whether you can reestablish that rapport the next time you meet, when there really is an agenda. Can you capture the magic of that first meeting, even while you get down to the nitty-gritty of business? Remember that your customer will go back to his own world, and everything will be different when you meet again. Will you have to spend half your time just reestablishing the trust you built up, especially now that the prospect has gone home and thought about what it was you really wanted?

One Last Question: Where Are All the Quotes?

By now you've probably noticed that this little chapter has very few quotes in little boxes to make the reading more enjoyable. That's because of one simple reason: no one, no matter how ancient or wise, can advise you on how to resolve this dilemma. It's a decision that you have to make yourself, based on everything you've learned until now: based on your gut, but also on your intellect. But whatever you decide – one meeting or two – there is one quote that should see you through, no matter what you decide.

> *"Sometimes you make the right decision;*
> *sometimes you make the decision right."*
> — Phillip C. McGraw

Chapter V

The Pitcher Takes the Mound

I study pitchers. I visualize pitches. That gives me a better chance every time I step into the box.

—Mark McGwire

ank Aaron once commented that, in theory at least, the batter should beat the pitcher every time. After all, "The pitcher has got only a ball. I've got a bat. So the percentage in weapons is in my favor ..." But in baseball – and in survival sales – we can turn that ball – or that product – into a formidable weapon.

There's another big difference too. In baseball, the pitcher has to decide whether to use a curveball, a screwball, a slider, a sinker, a knuckleball, or even a spitball. Does he start from the windup or the set? All those decisions have to be made just to psych out the batter. But in sales, you've already passed the big dilemma by deciding whether it's one meeting or two; all that's left is for you to make the pitch, and as we'll see, it's as easy as ABC (DEFG). In fact, anyone can pitch if they master a few simple steps. Just like in baseball, they're the very same steps that the pitcher has followed year after year, ever since he was a little boy practicing in the park with his dad. In baseball, as in sales, there are all sorts of pitches, but they all have the same basic stance, the same basic wind-up, the same basic follow-through.

So let's forget about curveballs and sliders and screwballs for now, and get right to the basics of every perfect sales pitch – the pitch that anyone would swing at. Unlike baseball, sales is not a game, and the salesperson and customer aren't rivals for glory. If anything, they have the perfect symbiotic relationship. They are there to help each other.

As It Is

The most important thing you should have learned during the entire ascertainment is exactly

> *"The pain I feel now is the happiness I had before."*
>
> — C. S. Lewis

where your customer is hurting. And every customer is hurting somewhere, especially in a down economy. During that first meeting (or the first part of this meeting), you empathized and felt their pain with them, so now it's time to show them that you listened. Begin your pitch by paraphrasing their current situation and reviewing the key points that they raised. Make it short by listing just their key points, but don't make it sweet by telling them how great things are. If anything, don't be afraid to rub a little salt in their wounds! When you over-emphasize the specific problems, the customer will begin to realize how important it is to find a solution.

Some people like to do this verbally, but I believe that writing shows commitment. It shows that you really listened to what your customers said, and gave serious thoughts to their needs. You are bringing them back to the magic of that first meeting, and drawing on the rapport you established then.

I find that the best way to review that meeting is to break it down into no more than five or six distinct points. Let's take Ellen's coffee shop, Aroma, as an example. After talking with her for half an hour, I learned that she's been in business for years and has a steady clientele, but also that the neighborhood has seen a lot of new offices open up, and that the staff at these new offices tends to favor the more familiar, "corporate chains" for their coffee and lunch. When I come back to Ellen to make my pitch, I bring her a sheet with the following points.

- Aroma has been a neighborhood institution for the past twenty years.

- Given the rising rent, Aroma must increase its business by 20 percent over the next six months.

- Aroma must draw in customers from this new group of upwardly mobile staff people that are now working in the area.

- They don't know that Aroma not only has an extensive selection of coffees, but also has a great selection of sandwiches on fresh bread and croissants baked on the premises.

- Few customers are taking advantage of Aroma's delivery service.

- While there are many potential customers out there for a brisk lunchtime coffee trade, Aroma is not winning their business. Instead, all these potential customers are frequenting the competitors instead! (You want to pour a little salt in the wound.)

Turning to Ellen, I ask her if I got everything right. She nods her head gratefully. I may not have been the first person she told about her problems, but I am the first person who listened to her. If I had any problem reestablishing rapport, the fact that I took the time to write all that down indicates to her that I care. Now I'm ready to pull out my next piece of paper.

Of course, it is also possible that Ellen might say, "No, that's not right." When this happens there are two possibilities to take into consideration. It is entirely possible that the prospect lied, for any one of a number of reasons. You may have caught the wrong person, who didn't really know the ins and outs of the business, or you may have found someone who got so tired of all the bad salespeople pounding on the door that they decided to pull a fast one on the next "sucker" that came through it. Of course, if you think about it, they're the real suckers, because they lost out on a chance to deal with you and really pull their business up by its bootstraps. Nevertheless, there is nothing you can do right now, except try to win back their faith and trust. Can you get them to really open up? If so, forget about the pitch you came in with and begin the ascertainment process again to identify where they really are hurting. And if you can't do that … Next!

Of course, there is also the chance that you didn't really hear what the customer was telling you. New salespeople especially have a hard time mastering the listening skills essential to a good ascertainment process. Here too there is no good reason to continue with the pitch that you were planning. But that does not mean that you should make a quick dash for the door. Instead, this is a great opportunity to improve your listening skills. What did you get right? What did you get wrong? What you are doing is restarting the ascertainment process, only this time you will be much more in tune with what the customer is saying.

As It Should Be

Assuming that your "As It Is" bullets accurately reflect the current state of Ellen's business, it's

> *"A map of the world that does not include Utopia is not worth even glancing at."*
> — Oscar Wilde

time to show Ellen what Aroma could become … with a little help from you, the salesperson. If she were my prospect, I would now take out a second piece of paper with all of those bullets shown clearly resolved. In fact, this second sheet contains the exact same bullets but with the addition of where I think she would like to be six months from now – and it just so happens that this coincides with where I believe I can get her. To show how this works, I'll put it in a chart:

As It Is Today	As It Should Be 6 months from now
Long-established neighborhood institution.	Aroma is the leader among loal coffee shops.
Increases in fixed costs mean an increase in revenue needed.	Aroma's business has increased 30 percent.
New customers needed.	Aroma is the leading hang-out for local businesspeople.
Selection and bakery unknown to public.	Aroma is the popular lunch spot for local businesspeople.
Delivery service unknown to public.	Offices are ordering delivery services so that employees don't have to leave for coffee.
Corporate chains drawing away Aroma's potential customers.	Aroma is drawing the clientele it needs to grow the business.

I've shown Ellen the future as if it is the present, and offered her a chance to the solve the problems that are keeping her awake at night. By the way, I'm sure you've noticed that I haven't even entered the picture yet. This is still part of a review of the ascertainment process, and as you probably realize by now: until we've gotten our customers' needs and dreams down pat, say *absolutely nothing* about your product! So right now the focus is still on Ellen's little coffee shop and the enormous potential it has – instead of cream and sugar what it needs is a little help from the service you offer, because you're solving problems, not selling a product.

Getting over the Rainbow

Have you ever really thought about a rainbow? An old saying claims that

> *"Be thou the rainbow in the storms of life."*
> — Lord Byron

it takes both rain and sunshine to make one. We have the rain (As It Is) and we have the sunshine (As It Should Be). So now it's up to you to be the rainbow.

In case you haven't realized it yet, that's exactly what sales is all about: being the bridge between rain and sunshine, pain and reward, as it is and as it should be. And talking about "as it should be," that's exactly what you should be – that bridge, or better yet that rainbow, adding a dash of color into your customer's business. After all, even the great Wizard of Oz was really a transplanted salesman.

Who Are You Anyways?

You're the rainbow, so it's time to remind the customer of that. Take a moment to pause, and remind the

> *"One good anecdote is worth a volume of biography."*
> — William Ellery Channing

customer who you are. But keep it short. They're not here to listen to a glowing – and interminable – list of your company's achievements. You're here to solve their problems, so remind them briefly why you think you're qualified. But do it briefly. In fact, this entire part of the pitch should be no longer than this segment.

There are a few common mistakes that salespeople make at this stage of the pitch. While you do want to talk about your company or product, you don't want to pull out a PR kit, stuffed with charts, graphs, and binders covering every detail of your business for the past twenty years. It's boring. You don't even want to focus on your company's greatest achievements if they have nothing to do with your customer's business. For example, in newspaper advertising, you may actually great pride in the fact that your paper has won a Pulitzer Prize for its coverage of some event or other, but unless Ellen is selling coffee there, it will probably have very little impact on her actual business needs. If, on the other hand, your "Lifestyle" section is read by a growing demographic of young professionals eager to find out what your town has to offer, you should certainly make her aware of that. Show the best that you can offer, but *only* when you can also show how that makes you the long-awaited rainbow that can lead your prospect's business to the pot of gold that's waiting at the end of it.

Unfortunately, too many media companies that I work with have the bad habit of putting all their research in a single book, together with all the information about each of their specific products. The salesperson is then chained to this book, even though most of its information is irrelevant to any particular customer. This only makes it difficult for them to highlight the precise product that they selected to solve the customer's particular problem. Therefore, if you do favor a one-call approach, make sure that you have all your research and information separated by product in individual folders. Know where each specific folder is in your binder, so that you only pull the right one out at the right moment.

Being able to focus on a specific solution is yet another reason why I favor the two-call approach. If, for example, I was talking to Ellen, I'd certainly like to show her why our audience is identical to hers. In media advertising this is actually quite simple because we have a myriad of niche products suitable for diverse audiences. As I like to tell my clients, "It doesn't matter if it's the most popular section. You still do not advertise a shop selling baby gifts in the sports section of your paper!" And that's not just true about newspapers either. If you are selling office furniture, don't brag that your desks can be assembled and taken apart in 20 minutes flat, if the company you're selling to hasn't moved a piece of furniture since they entered their current workspace, back in the 1960s. Rather, you must find your niche product, and once you find it, stick to it!

The Proposal

This is the moment we've all been waiting for. Now you can present the ideal solution to your customer's

> *"Our major obligation is not to present slogans for solutions."*
> — Edward R. Murrow

problem. Lay it out on a single piece of paper, so that it is concise and legible. Add both your logo and your customer's logo, but make sure your customer's logo is much larger. Most of all, lay the proposal out so that it addresses the points you listed above. Show how your particular solution leads from Column A to Column B – from As It Is to As It Should Be.

The Proposal: Take Two

If I am taking a two-call approach, I will have two copies of my presentation with me. The first is the presentation on single pages, which I share with my prospect, one page at a time, as I go through my pitch. The second presentation, a bound version of all those pages, is only given to the customer after I have finished. The reason for this is simple. If I give him the bound presentation first, the customer will usually ignore me while he flips through the presentation to find the price.

In media sales one of these pages is what we called a "spec," or "speculative ad." This is a mock up of a concept that will actually solve their problems. Unfortunately, too many media salespeople forget this. They are so busy pontificating about column inches, placement, or banner position on a web page that they forget that it is the actual words in the ad which solve their customer's problem. The spec is essential to media sales, whether it is a print ad, an online ad, or both. It is a chance to enlist the real features of the product to show how it helps the customer go from As It Is to As It Should Be.

Providing a spec also has another advantage. When any customer sees an ad for their business, the first thing that they usually do is pull out a pen and start "correcting" it. Bingo! This tells you that they've already taken ownership of it, and are only tweaking it now to meet their precise specifications. In fact, we call this the Copy Close, which is part of the hypnotic closing process that we will discuss later. In brief, however, there is no clearer buying signal than a customer taking ownership. Once that happens, you've already clinched the deal, even if the customer doesn't realize it yet!

So, now that you've presented your proposal and specs, you can finally get to the price, which must be stated loud and proud!
Having said all this, I should note that some old-school salespeople suggest putting the price at the very top of the proposal. Some people using this approach may even incorporate the price into the title: *How the Aroma Café Will Grow Its Business with a $1300 Investment!* The logic is that this gets the customer's biggest concern out of the way, rather than have him worry about it during your entire presentation. Personally, I have never been a big advocate of this approach, and prefer to justify the cost before I actually state it.

I've spent years selling media, and to this day I think that it's an incredible marketing tool. It's a means of reaching hundreds of thousands of people with a message about a product that you really believe in. Infomercials are another great way to spread the news of some great new innovation that will make people's lives everywhere so much easier. But that's advertising, not sales. With all the media tools at our disposal – skywriting, newspapers, radio, television, the internet, or even some poor guy in a chicken suit parading around with a sandwich-board ad – there is nothing quite as powerful as the personal connection between prospect and salesperson, or, as it should really be called, the person with the problem, and the person with the solution. It's one of life's little ironies that we are grateful to doctors for solving our health problems and to accountants for solving our tax problems, but we forget how often salespeople solve people's problems too.

Chapter 5

It Ain't Over Yet!

By now, you must think that you're finally ready for the close! Before you do that though, pull out your

> *"I have always thought the actions of men the best interpreters of their thoughts."*
> — John Locke

calendar and get ready with an action plan. Face it! No matter how great your proposal may look, there's still one thing that's worrying your customer: How does he know that you can deliver? History is full of snake-oil salesmen, who said all the right words and made all the right promises. How does he know that you're not one of them? How can he be assured that you can be trusted to take his hard-earned money?

That's where the action plan fits in. With your calendar in hand, begin the process by showing your customer a timeline. In media sales, I am always armed with blank calendars showing the weeks of the month, but with no dates on them. I then write at the top of each calendar the name of the month and a start date for each week, so that I can physically show them when the product will impact them. If I am selling newspaper advertising, I'll put X's on the days that the ad will run in the paper. If I am selling radio advertising, with a certain number of commercials per day, I'll put numbers in the boxes representing the days that their commercials run. With Internet sales, when I am selling impressions per week, I'll write the number of impressions in bold letters, and add an arrow across the whole week. Regardless of the particular media, what I am showing is a physical commitment to the time that is devoted to the product.

But this is no less relevant to any other B2B sales. The calendar should show when the new copier will be delivered, when the installation team will come, or when the office space will be ready for occupancy. In other words, you are showing your customer a simple plan of how the business will take place over time. But that is not all the calendar is used for. Also mark on it when you plan to have your follow-up meetings to provide your customers with service. Sales does not end with delivery. Your customers will be much more at ease if they realize that you plan to continue working with them to ensure that all their expectations are met.

If the customer begins to comment on the dates, you are ready to jump right to the close! After all, why would a potential customer discuss meeting dates, unless they have already taken ownership of your product? This is yet another example of hypnotic selling. All that remains is to ask a few open choice questions that will bring the sale to its conclusion: "Do we start on Monday or Thursday? Do you want b/w or color?" (the Alternative Choice close again!).

With that information, the next step is simple. Fill out the order form, get a signature, and get out! You have closed the sale!

As Easy as ABC

Do you remember how, at the beginning of this chapter, I said that pitching can be as easy as ABC

> *"Success is that old ABC: Ability, Breaks, and Courage."*
> — Charles Luckman

(DEFG)? I bet you were wondering to yourself why I was showing off my skills by reciting the alphabet? Actually, the ABCs are a great way to remember everything we talked about until now, so let's go through them, letter by letter:

- **A = Ascertainment:** Find out your customers' precise needs, and see if you have just the solution for them.

- **B = Break:** Now that you know those needs, you will probably want to arrange a second meeting for you to make your pitch (or, if you're taking a one-meeting approach, wind down before you turn the corner).

- **C = Current Situation:** Review your customer's situation As It Is, starting with gain and ending with pain!

- **D = Desirable Situation:** Show your customer where she wants to be and where you want to bring her (As It Should Be).

- **E = Ego:** By now the customer is probably wondering why you think you can get them there, so offer some targeted information about your product that justifies your ability to take them from their current situation (**C**) to the desirable situation (**D**) through the company you represent. Just don't get carried away: remember, this is about your customer, not you!

- **F = For Sale:** Show them your proposal and your price.

- **G = Go for It!:** Break out your calendar, action plan, and order form, because now it's time to close!

With these seven steps, you don't need curveballs and sliders and screwballs. In fact, you probably don't even want them. What you want is your customer to hit a home run, and for you to get to the close. And that means you want the easiest pitch of all!

Chapter VI

Openings:
The Chapter You Won't Need[1]

Windows never open themselves, especially windows of opportunity!

— Mike Blinder

Most people expect a book about sales to end with a chapter called closings. Not me. In fact, I believe that the whole paradigm of "closing" must change if we reallly intend to survive in sales. Closing is too final, too conclusive, too terminal. It makes it seem like "the end is nigh!" when in sales, a successful close should be a start: the start of a successful business relationship, the beginning of new prospecting possibilities, and the launch of an entirely unexplored succession of opportunities.

But just like any creaky old window that remained shut all winter, the first time you open the window of opportunity you may have to add a bit of pressure, or better yet, to make it open smoothly, you may have to oil the tracks and hinges. Sometimes you even have to find the key that was put away a long time ago. It takes some effort, but the effort is worth it if you finally get that burst of air, that cool evening breeze, that fresh new business.

So rather than get into the mechanics of closing – plenty of great salespeople have done that before me[2] – I'd rather talk about the mechanics of opening, because that's precisely what survival in sales is all about, especially in a down economy. Like John D. Rockefeller

---

1   You really may not need this chapter! If you have followed all of the previous steps, and delivered the perfect pitch, very often you won't even have to resort to the closing techniques mentioned here, because your customer will have already agreed to buy! If anything, this chapter on Closing is a Chapter of Last Resort. It is only for those annoying instances when you have done absolutely everything right, but there still is some invisible mental block that prevents the advertiser from saying yes.

2   See Appendix B for a list of some great books precisely about that.

before me, "I always tried to turn every disaster into an opportunity." The down economy is our golden opportunity!

The Window Washer

Obviously, not every window can be opened that easily. Zig Ziglar talks about "gorilla dust,"

> *"The Wright brothers flew through a smoke screen of impossibility."*
> — Charles F. Kettering

the bluffing and posturing that some businessmen use to obscure their true intentions, when you come to make a close. It's based on how two wild gorillas fight, by scooping up fistfuls of earth and dust and throwing them in the air to create an enormous smokescreen. That way, they're not really fighting against each other but rather against a cloud of nothing that obscures each gorilla's view of the other.

As anyone who's dealt with a jammed window will tell you, the first thing to do when you want to get it open is to clean it off. Get rid of all that accumulated dust and determine whether the humming and hawing really some has substance to it. Is it an obstacle or is it a smokescreen: is it a *condition* or is it just an *objection?*

There's no use fighting a condition. In other words, if the person you're meeting with finally admits that he simply can't make a decision, this is not someone you should spend much time sitting with. Either use that person to get to the real decision-maker – a tactic I am wary of, because he should have sent you there sooner – or beat a hasty retreat and move on. Alternately, you might hear your prospect effuse profusely over your product and admit that they would love to buy it … if they weren't on the verge of bankruptcy. Here too, the best path leads to the door. You may be there to help save his business, but sometimes it's too late.

An objection is an entirely different challenge. It is the proverbial "gorilla dust," that we spoke about earlier: "I'd love to buy an ad in your paper, but I'd like to wait until next month to see how well our sales go by then." In other words, he is throwing you a bone just to get you out of his office. The problem is that his claim is illogical: if his business is truly down, why would he want to wait to see if it goes down any further.

Unfortunately, that doesn't really matter. When a customer has no real reason to proceed, one excuse is as good as the next. The fact that his mother-in-law is coming to visit for a month is just as valid an excuse *to him* as not being able to afford your service. An objection is smoke, not substance.

But then the question is obvious. If objections are little more than smokescreens, why make them in the first place? If the business you're pitching to does have a genuine problem and you are offering them the perfect solution, why would they even think of turning it down? Do businesses really have a subconscious need to remain stuck in a rut? Perhaps. Let's face it: the devil you know is better than the devil you don't know. We all fear change, and while Helen Keller said, "When one door of happiness closes, another opens," she added that, "often we look so long at the closed door' – or in our case, window – "that we don't see the one that has been opened for us."

What should you do? Well first, what shouldn't you do? Never, ever argue with your customer. Don't force the window because you may break the glass. Don't counter negative energy with even more negative energy, because you may end up shattering the rapport. Instead, consider what Ueshiba Morihei, a great martial artist and the founder of Aikido, taught to his students: "If your opponent strikes with fire, counter with water ... Water, by its nature, never collides with or breaks against anything. On the contrary, it swallows up any attack harmlessly." Let him vent and get it out of his system, and then continue to move on. By becoming water you can douse the enthusiasm behind even the fieriest objections.

I've seen this in my life time and again. As a sixteen-year-old, I worked in Radio Shack, where I sometimes dealt with disgruntled customers. The latest fad at the time was CB radio, soon to go the way of the dodo and the 8-track cassette, but back then just about everyone was buying them, excited by the technological progress. It was almost like having a phone in your car!

Until one morning a customer walked in who was, in a word, less than happy with his purchase. In fact, from the way he was fuming I could tell he spent the entire night calculating at what angle he would slam his new radio down on the counter to get the maximum effect. With a growl and a grunt, he roared, "What is this piece of …"

"Sir," I said with my sweetest adolescent smile. "Would you like a cash refund on that?"

"What? Sure, yeah! Thanks." His grumble had turned to a mumble. His negative energy had dissipated. In the end, we had a very nice discussion, and I ended up saving the sale.

There are always hurdles that must be overcome. The first thing to do is isolate them, and make sure that they are the only hurdles left. In other words, there's no use wasting time answering objections that do not exist. In fact, it may actually be downright dangerous. "I know you don't like the color, but before I address that let me talk about why we're so expensive," will only get your customer wondering if you really are so expensive.

Isolate the objection instead, and make sure that it really is the only objection hindering the close. Is the color really the problem, or is it a roundabout way for the customer to tell you that it is too expensive. "I understand that you don't like the color, but I want to make sure that you are perfectly fine with the price, the delivery schedule, and all of the issues that this resolves." If there are other problems out there, you really do need to know about them, so that you don't address the wrong problem. If you're going to leap over the hurdles, make sure that they are the right hurdles.

While watching the Beijing Olympics, I was amazed by the prowess of the hurdlers. Not only did they have to dash down the track, but they had to do it while getting past at least ten annoying obstacles. Always thinking about my job, I thought, "What a wonderful metaphor for the training I do, helping people overcome objections!" But when I told a friend about it, he took the wind out of my dreams of an Olympic Selling competition: "I used to like the hurdles too, until I thought: Why not just go around them?" In fact, that's exactly what we do when confronting a smokescreen – we simply go around it!

If, after all that, your window of opportunity still remains jammed and you can't go around it by opening another window, you may have no choice but to isolate the problem. Is it a hinge that is rusty or a runner that is stuck? Is it an old fashioned approach to doing business ("We've been typesetting manually for a hundred years. Why would we need a computer to do that?"), or is there something else you can't see that is clogging up the decision ("Yes, it's great, but I like to take my time deciding things. Why don't we talk again in three months?").

If this is the case, the best thing to do is to rephrase the objection. With some carefully wording – and wording is everything – you can show your prospect how ridiculous it is. For instance, if the prospect is someone who likes to take his time before deciding, you might simply repeat back exactly what he said to you in a valiant effort to understand it: "Before we even go any further, let me see if I understand what you're saying. You agree that your business is losing money and that the ad campaign I am proposing will help you turn that around, *but* you'd also like to wait three months before doing anything about it. Is that correct?" Or, "Before we even go any further, you say that your business needs to be more efficient in order to compete, and that the brand new graphics program that I'm offering will save you significant man-hours and money, *but* you haven't ever used it before, and you're not sure you want to start now. Did I understand you correctly?" When asked with empathy and genuine disbelief, who could possibly say no?

Using the Right Language

Of course, you have to make sure you're using the right tools, or in the case of sales, speaking the same language. In our culture,

> *"He who wants to persuade should put his trust not in the right argument, but in the right word. The power of sound has always been greater than the power of sense."*
> — Joseph Conrad

the language we choose can be everything. The German entrepreneur Karl Albrecht once said, "Change your language and you change your thoughts," so change the tone of the language you use to convert your customer's perception. English has plenty of "four-letter words," and so does sales, chief among them *sell* and *cost*. It even has a three-letter word: *buy*; and a six-letter word: *dollar*. Take them out of your vocabulary when speaking to a customer, and replace them with far friendlier words, such as *invest*, *approve*, *agreement*, and *opportunity*. After all, I'm sure you'll all agree that offering a customer a chance to "invest in this product" is much more conducive to sales than "Do you want to buy it?"

But the language of sales is far more complicated than that. In this language, we never say *if* but *when*: "When you buy this product …" not "If you buy this product …" It speaks in absolutes, about products that *will*, rather than products that *might*. If this sounds a little exaggerated, remember that this is a language that uses the most vivid colors, tastes, sounds, and smells to describe its products. It's a language where every challenge has solutions and every need is met, where the active tense is the future tense of As It Should Be.

Hypnotic Selling

We've all seen hypnotists at work, either on stage or on television. But in addition to their entertainment value,

> *"Ads are not meant for conscious consumption. They are intended as subliminal pills for the subconscious, in order to exercise an hypnotic spell."*
> — Marshall McLuhan

hypnosis and subliminal suggestion are crucial to the sales process, regardless of what you're selling. In fact, even the most basic search on the internet for the word *hypnosis* alone will lead you to countless sites and books about this very topic. They are worth looking into.

Of course, you should never expect to get your customers falling asleep and pretending they're a chicken before you close a deal with them. While that may be fun as a parlor trick, it really is not what hypnosis is about. According to the American Society of Clinical Hypnosis (ASCH), it is actually, "a state of inner absorption, concentration, and focused attention"[3] – precisely the state we want our customers to be in: concentrated and focused so that they absorb the value of our products. As the ASCH continues, "In a state of concentrated attention, ideas and suggestions that are compatible with what the patient wants seem to have a more powerful impact on the mind." What could possibly be more compatible than helping customers solve the problems that they want to see solved?

As any of the books on the topic will tell you, the way to achieve hypnotic selling is twofold. You must have the trust of your customer – the trust achieved through rapport and good eye contact, but you must also use the right language to introduce subliminal suggestions. In the previous section, we mentioned the use of terms like "When you buy," instead of "If you buy." It is all about the power of suggestion, and when presented properly, you customers will "take suggestion as a cat laps milk."[4]

Hypnotic sales are an ideal way of avoiding the obstacles before the close. During the entire pitch, speak to your customers as if they already own the product. In media sales, foster that sense of ownership with specs – speculative advertisements that they can correct – because once they start correcting a spec, they are already post-agreement. As we mentioned in the previous chapter, the action plan that you present

---

3   See their website at http://www.asch.net/genpubinfo.htm.
4   William Shakespeare, *The Tempest* II, 1. Interestingly, the quote itself has a business angle to it as well. It continues, "They'll tell the clock to any hour that we say befits the business."

is an essential part of hypnotic closing. Once you have mastered hypnotic closing techniques, you'll be able to tunnel through even the most obstinate objections, rather than struggling up and over the hump. When it comes to choosing the words that will persuade, remember that "Words are also actions."[5]

Closing and Opening: The Final Push

Like hypnotic selling, so much has been written about the techniques of closing, that it seems a pity to reiterate them

> *"About 15 percent of one's financial success is due to one's technical knowledge, and about 85 percent is due to skill in human engineering, to personality, and the ability to lead people."*
> — Dale Carnegie

here. By now, the main point should be clear. It is not the "friend," the "natural," or the "expert" who will survive in sales. Sales is a science of human engineering, where we use the power of rapport to lead, not only for our own sake, but for the sake of the people we are leading – the customers who need our help.

But even with those few basic building blocks, sales can be as diverse as the people who buy and as you, the people who sell. Each salesperson, each customer, and certainly each product comes together to form an infinite variation of possibilities, just like three colors—red, yellow, and blue—can combine in different ways to form the infinite spectrum of the rainbow. Luckily, we have a few specific "formulas" to help us reach any color we want. And in sales we have formulas too, so that we get our desired outcome.

There are ten basic closing techniques, many of them as old as the very first salesperson, selling a woolly mammoth hide for 6 spears. Briefly, they are:

- **The Puppy Dog Close**, like its name suggests, probably began at a pet store. Rather than discussing the household benefits of owning a dog or how pet ownership teaches children responsibility, the salesman

---

5   Ralph Waldo Emerson.

placed the puppy in the little girl's arms and it was love at first lick. "Daddy, I want him!" How dare anyone take that puppy away from her! But the Puppy Dog Close has come a long way, and is now found in just about any sales environment. Cars salesmen use it when they get their customers behind the wheel "for a spin." In media we certainly use it when we present a mock up "spec" of a stunning ad or website, with the customer's logo prominently placed … and all it takes to make it yours is to sign on the dotted line! Can anyone say no?

In media sales, the Puppy Dog Close is perfect for selling online advertising. What I like to do is place an ad spec online on some webpage during the time that I am in my meeting. The customer is suddenly thrilled that the ad can be seen by millions of potential visitors. Of course, if he wants it to stay there, he must first sign on the dotted line.

Like many of these closes, the Puppy Dog Close is actually another form of hypnotic selling. When you offer your customer a spec, you will often see them bring out a pencil and begin to mark it up, moving the logo, making slight changes to the language, or adding additional graphic elements. While some people might be discouraged by this, it is actually the best sign of all. Suddenly, they've taken ownership and the spec is now "theirs," using what we earlier called the Copy Close (which is a form of the Puppy Dog Close). In fact, I would probably encourage them to mark it up as much as possible, because it has become their ad.

Having said that, I should note that one variation of this close encourages the salesperson to argue with the customer about some of the changes. The point isn't to prove that you have a better sense of aesthetics than her – in fact, you should always let your customers have the final word. But by defending her changes, the customer is signaling to you that this is now hers and no longer yours.

• **The Hot Button Close** is a way of focusing on those very benefits that the customer finds irresistible. "Sure it is a little more expensive than you originally planned," you mumble, "but can you imagine ALL THE NEW BUSINESS THAT THIS CAMPAIGN WILL BRING YOU!" you intone, in a rising crescendo. When you highlight the favorite selling points, the objections will seem pretty meaningless.

The classic example of this is the realtor who leads a couple through a house that is desperately in need of repairs. The wife loves the garden, especially an old apple tree that reminds her of her childhood home. The husband, meanwhile, is calculating the hours it will take to get the house in shape. Conscious of this, the realtor walks into the most dismal room of all, the kitchen, followed by the glowing wife and the grumbling husband. But before anyone can say a thing, he quickly draws back the blinds and says, "And look at this magnificent view of the garden. It's almost like the window was a frame for that apple tree." Plumbing, tiling, electricity aside, he realized that the tree was the hot button that would sell this house.

• **The Invitational Close** is a call to action, reminiscent of a high school pep rally: "Let's do this right now!" You can almost hear the band playing in the background as you march off to clinch the deal.

• **The Sharp Angle Close** turns the customer's objections into the actually selling point. Do you remember our customer back in Ascertainment, who wasn't that thrilled with the green cocktail dress: "I think I would prefer it in black." But our intrepid saleswoman was ready for her: "Black? Yes, that would look great on you! I think we have one over here." In other words, what she was really saying was, "If we have it in black will you buy it?" Objection dismissed! On to the close!

• **The Switch Places Close** is especially useful when customers come up with all sorts objections so as not to buy the product. "If I was the customer and you were the salesperson, what would you say to get me to buy it?" The logic behind this close is simple: as convincing a salesperson as you may be, there is no one who can convince a customer better than the customer himself.

• **The Summary Close** is the most basic close of all. You simply go over all of the customer's needs (you should have the As It Is sheet handy), followed by how you meet those needs. Wouldn't it then make perfect sense for the customer to buy your product?

• **The Ben Franklin Close** comes straight from the desk of Benjamin Franklin, who once described how he made all his decisions. He drew up a table listing the pros and cons, and simply tallied them up. Of course, in a sales situation, you'll be helping the customer create that table by highlighting all the pros as to why your product is the perfect solution.

• **The Alternative Choice Close** is based on the assumption that the customer already decided to buy your product ... whether he actually knows it or not. "Would you like to start on Wednesday or Friday?" Regardless of what the answer is, the customer has agreed to start. One of my favorite variations on this was told to me by the late Alan Cymberg, an inspirational salesman like few others. With an ever so slight hint of irreverence, he would ask his customers: "Would you like to start now, or would you rather hear more?" Getting out of the close was never an option!

• **The Reverse Close** takes the higher price option as its starting point, allowing you the flexibility to generously lower your price. Imagine how grateful the customer will be when you come up with an even better offer.

- **The "Columbo" (Doorknob) Close** is based on Peter Falk's character Columbo, but also on the premise that objections (but not conditions) are really a smokescreen that is intended to test your perseverance and mettle. If the objections can't be overcome, let the customer win! Head to door, and he will feel like he beat you, but just as his guard is down spin around and say, "One last thing!" While your customer fumbles to get his guard back up, you can move ahead to the final close.

In over twenty years of sales, I've had an opportunity to use each and every one of these closes, both individually and in various combinations. Like the basic colors, they combine well together to offer an infinite assortment of possibilities, and make it possible for you to close under even the most trying circumstances.

One Last Thing

The biggest mistake we often make is thinking that history begins with us, or that the challenges our generation faces somehow overwhelm those faced by our forebears. In our current down economy we tend to forget that some elderly people still remember life during the Great Depression and certainly during Black Monday of 1988 and the dot. com bust of the early 1990s – three events from the last century. In this new internet era, we often forget the enormous revolution that television, radio, and the telephone all played in shaping our society. It's strange because our parents and grandparents often do remember life without them.

Sure, the world is changing quickly thanks to all the amazing new technologies that have emerged in the past one hundred years. But Buckminster Fuller was absolutely wrong when he claimed that we'd be living in geodesic domes somewhere on the ocean floor, with no shopping or genuine social interactions to keep us busy. As a society, we still like to do all these things in the traditional way, and if you don't believe me, go to Mall of the Americas. All of the latest technological advances are only there to help us behave as humans behaved for thousands of years. People wrote letters long before they wrote email; people read books before they had televisions; people spoke long before they had telephones; and people did business long before they learned to shop online. In fact, some of the earliest writings we find in cuneiform tablets from Sumer contain precisely that – business – people trading a sheep for a bushel of corn, or an amphora of wine for a half dozen pigeons.

Sales has come a long way since then. The alphabet, currency, paper, printing, and yes, even the internet, have made it easier for us to do business. No matter how advanced they seemed at the time, none of these technological wonders has managed to eliminate business as an essential human transaction. Technologies may change, but business hasn't – even in an internet era. In fact, I'm convinced that if I were to translate this book into Sumerian and hand it out on clay tablets in the marketplace of Sumer, the successful merchants would know exactly what I'm talking about, even if phrases like the "Columbo Close" would stymie them.

The problem is that in this internet era, some people think that since one thing has changed, everything else must change along with it. Things have certainly changed, it's true, but some things will always remain the same, no matter how quickly we get our mail or our news. So rather than banging our heads against a wall and trying to reinvent the wheel, we should be taking a much more careful look to see how our tried and true sales techniques continue to offer the best possible solutions. After all, we're no longer selling sheep and corn, just like we're no longer sending our bills on clay tablets in cuneiform. We sell solutions, and people always need those, no matter what era they live in. And most of all, people will be people, no matter what era they live in too.

Don't you agree?

Chapter VII

Being the Best!

We are what we repeatedly do. Excellence, then, is not an act but a habit.

—Aristotle

For some people, the easiest thing about sales is finding excuses for why they're not selling. All they have to do is to open the paper or turn on the news: "Will you take a look at the economy! How am I possibly supposed to do well when businesses everywhere are struggling to stay open?" It's the same old story. When in doubt, blame the government, the economy, the weather, or some other distant force that you can't control. Then there are the "personal excuses": "I get no support from my boss! The competition has a much better product and at half the price! My clients have no idea of what they want." I could go on and on. I've heard them all a million times in many countries and in multiple languages from the salespeople I've been asked to train, coach, and mentor.

Do you know what? Each of those excuses probably has some merit. We are in a down economy, with businesses closing all around us. Your boss may be a gigantic jerk, the competition may be cheaper, and maybe your client has problems deciding what color socks to put on in the morning, never mind making crucial decisions for the multi-million dollar business that his grandfather left him. Life is so unfair!

But!

They are still just excuses, and until you stop blaming them for all your problems, they will continue to plague you! Get over it! Kipling once said that there are "forty million reasons for failure, but not a single excuse." I would add, "unless the excuse is you!" Rather than getting dragged down by every imaginable excuse, make the decision once and for all that you will not be bogged down by your problems. Instead you are going to conquer them!

Our Aspirations Are Our Possibilities!

Remember that just about everyone faced tough times at one point

> *"Difficulty is the excuse history never accepts."*
> — Edward R. Murrow

or another. I know I did. In fact, twenty years ago I was convinced that my life was in a tailspin. I had just gone through a miserable divorce, my credit cards were all maxed out, and this was having an impact on my numbers. I was a wreck! But once wallowing in self-pity got to be a bore, I decided to take a self-help course, and found myself a mentor who turned my life around – in a single night!

At one of the sessions I attended, Ivan Burnell asked us to pull out a piece of paper and write down where we want to be ten years from now.[1] Actually, it's a pretty common exercise, but the way we did it had a special little twist. We were told to "Write it as if you own it!" We were supposed to make that future ours!

I still have that piece of paper. The ink is faded, and the paper is starting to show signs of aging, but none of that really matters. It's the words that are remarkable.

- I <u>have</u> a career in training/speaking (*the underline is in the original*) – ✓

- I am making no less than $X per year (*there's a number in the original too, which I have exceeded many times over*) – ✓

- I travel to exciting places when I want to, doing #1 – ✓

- I am famous among that class of people that know my work and business – ✓

- I have free time when I want it to travel, relax, and learn – ✓

---

1   For more about Ivan Burnell, see http://yesfactor.com/.

Twenty years later, I still keep the note from Ivan Burnell's self-help course. It was a personal "As It Should Be" statement for my life.

Back then, it all seemed pretty darn impossible, but with hindsight I realize that Samuel Johnson was right. Our aspirations really are our possibilities, if only we choose to make them that.

Fake It Till You Make It!

How many psychiatrists does it take to change a light bulb? One, but it has to really want to change! Or, perhaps, more

> *"There is nothing wrong with change if it is in the right direction."*
> — Winston Churchill

simply put: To make things work, you have to really want to change! Do you *really* want to change?

For most people, there is no easy answer. Change can be intimidating, and plenty of people live by the saying, "Better the devil you know than the devil you don't." You may decide that change is too risky, even in a down economy, even if your numbers are stuck in a rut. People like that can take comfort in the words of a French nobleman, the Comte d'Artois (later King Charles X), who admitted that "It is *not* necessary to change; Survival is *not* mandatory."

But if survival does appeal to you, consider what changes you must make now to break free of the circle you're trapped in. Envision what you can become, and start to act the part. To be a winner, you have to act like a winner, and if you act like a winner, people will think of you as a winner. So visualize what life will be like once you've succeeded, and start behaving as if you're already there. Pretty soon everyone will pick up on the little cues you leave about the new you, and start paving your way to success.

Visualize success every time you face a problem, and you'll see how quickly the problem disappears. It can be as mundane as trying to find a parking space on a crowded city street. Before I get there, I've already started visualizing what the perfect parking space will be, and sure enough, believe it or not, I'll usually find that parking space waiting for me. And whenever I have a "do or die" meeting, instead of running through all the possible outcomes, I just visualize one – the best one – and make it mine! Then, when I do attend the meeting, all that I am actually doing is going through the motions on my way to success.

On the Other Hand ...

On the other hand, there are plenty of people who are committed to failure, no matter what they do. In fact,

> *"Men do not stumble over mountains, but over molehills."*
> — Samuel Butler

with all the self-help books out there, I sometimes wonder if people would buy *How to Fail in Sales: A B2B Guide*. Not that anyone really wants to fail, but if you get caught up in any of the following pitfalls, you have no chance of surviving. By the way, as you go through this list, I am sure you'll notice that nowhere will you find even the slightest reference to a bad boss or a bad economy. In fact, they're all about the salesperson – you!

• **Lack of belief in yourself:** If you don't believe in yourself, no one else will believe in you either. The worst salespeople are the ones who convince themselves that they won't make the close, even before they make the pitch. So get out there and convince yourself by saying "I can do it!" Repeat it to yourself again and again, in front of a mirror and in front of the prospect's door. This ability to believe in myself was probably the most important lesson that I learned from Ivan Burnell. At his self-help class he shared his mantra with us, and it has since become my mantra too: "I am important. So is everyone else. I will never use my importance to put someone else down, and I will *never allow their importance to put me down.*" That's exactly the attitude a salesperson needs. When approaching a customer, regardless of whether it's the head of a multi-billion dollar corporation or the senior editor of a small local newspaper, go in there as an equal. You'll find that they will respect you more when you respect yourself!

- **Lack of belief in your product:** If you can't even convince yourself that your product is worth every penny, how can you possibly convince your customers that it is a worthwhile investment? Nobody is that good of an actor, and nobody is that good of a liar either. So before you go out pitching your product, make sure that you fully believe in it, and if you need to resort to deceptions and half truths, it probably isn't worth it. After all, half a truth is a whole lie.

- **Lack of belief in your company:** This is no less serious than failing to believe in your product. If you don't trust the people you work for, why would you trust the service they provide, or better yet, why would your customer trust it? The real problem is that none of us wants to face up to our own sense of inadequacy, so we tend to pass the blame off on those nearest to us. That's why, if you find yourself skeptical of your company, you should ask yourself honestly who is really to blame for the problems you are having: your company or you? If it is your company's fault, perhaps you should be pounding the street, looking for another job. But if it is you, don't fool yourself into believing that it's your company's fault. Your company is just an easy target for you to cast the blame.

- **A poor image of sales and of your role as a salesperson:** It's not your fault. Salespeople can and do get a bad rap, largely because of the enormous number of bad salespeople out there. In fact, the bad salesperson has become iconic to our culture, whether it's Willie Loman or the sleazy used car salesman who appears all over the movies and television. Who can forget the Door-to-Door Salesman on Pee-wee Herman's *Playhouse* shouting, "I'm going door to door to make you this incredible offer!" or Pee-wee Herman's horrified response, "Salesman!" as he slams the door in his face.

It's no wonder that even we forget that sales can be one of the noblest professions. It's what keeps the whole economy churning and the free market in motion. RCA would never have made the effort to put a radio in every home and share news and entertainment with every American if they didn't see a profit in selling companies the advertising messages that came through those speakers. The first communications satellites would never have been sent into orbit if the networks hadn't been able to sell advertising around the programs they sought to beam back to Earth. Google would never have continued developing its product line making vast amounts of information accessible to every single person on the planet if it wasn't for their ability to sell advertising and make a profit. If there are bad salespeople – and I have no doubt there are – the down economy will siphon them off, so that only the best survive.

- **Lack of confidence in your ability to communicate with your customers:** It's all part of visualization – if you believe you can do it you definitely will, but then there's the flip side of that coin: if you don't believe you can do it, you won't! Especially when it comes to words: if you don't think you can get your point across clearly, the chances are that you won't. So practice your lines again and again. I do it every morning in the shower, and trust me: it sounds much better than even my finest arias. My inspiration in this is NBA Hall of Famer Ed Macauley, who once said, "When you are not practicing, remember, someone somewhere is, and when you meet him he will win." Survival sales is all about winning!

- **Lack of confidence in the "roller-coaster" of sales:** Let's face it. That's exactly what sales is – a roller-coaster of good days and bad days, good economies and bad economies, sky-high earnings and barely breaking even. Imagine the excitement when you're just about to make a close, only to have it pulled out from under you because of some ridiculous objection. It's always like that, and it will always be like that: steep climbs and spine-tingling descents. We all know people who prefer the safety of the merry-go-round, circling around the same old spot at a nice, leisurely trot.

But one thing people forget about sales is that unlike the average roller-coast, you can actually set the pace and decide how high and how fast you go. Sitting at a desk job is like riding the merry-go-round, following the same, circular route, day after day after day. And in the end, what do you get? A 5 percent raise at the end of the year to match the rising C-o-L index. It's a totally different ride in sales. You set the pace, and you can even set your salary, because the harder you work, the higher you climb, and the more money you get to take home. In sales, you're not just riding the roller coaster; you're actually operating it too! Of course, that brings us to our next point though:

- **Lack of confidence in your ability to really manage yourself:** That's because, even if you are accountable to a boss, in sales the first person you are really accountable to is you! You are constantly on the move, prospecting pitching, ascertaining, and closing. In short, you are a private contractor, given the honor of representing a fine product. So ask yourself honestly whether you have the self-discipline that's absolutely necessary to survive in sales. And if you decide that you really don't, then work out what it takes to get that discipline, and thank God for the guilt you must feel that you don't have it yet!

- **Lack of investment in yourself:** It's not enough to believe that you can do it. You have to make sure you look like you can too, whether it's through the car you drive, the suit you wear, or the way that you present yourself to others. But investing in yourself goes much farther than that, because when any of us takes a good look in the mirror, we'll always find some way that we can improve ourselves. So do it! Constantly examine yourself, identify the challenges you face, and design the strategies you need to overcome them. As in just about everything else in life, you can't begin to tackle a problem before you know what the problem is. And just as we tend to focus on our strengths, we also tend to gloss over our weaknesses.

Do you really believe in your product and your company, in your skills and in your ability to communicate? Does the emotional roller-coaster of sales make you queasy? Do you need help managing your time, so that you make the most of it? Most of all, are you ready to take the leap and make the changes you need? If you've answered *Yes!* sincerely and honestly, you've already taken the first, giant step. After that, everything else is easy. Self-improvement is a never-ending task, but the upside is that you're competing against yourself!

The Secret of Success

When I was young, my mother always told me, "Michael, life is choices, not

> *"Our aspirations are our possibilities."*
> — Robert Browning

chances." It's a lesson I always took to heart. Only one in a billion will win that lottery. The rest of the people who succeed in life are the people like you who choose to succeed, and are willing to do what it takes to get there. Anyone can dream when they're asleep. It's what we do to keep the dream alive when we're awake that determines whether we can make our dreams come true. So by all means set goals for yourself, but set a strategy too. Without a road map to success, it's easy to get lost along the way.

Who are the truly great salespeople, the people with the clearest road map to success, who will reach their destination no matter what obstacles they encounter along the way? They are the people who have a healthy good dose of each of the following ten qualities:

Know Thy Product!

Yes, I said many pages
ago that simply knowing
a product inside and out

> *"For knowledge too is itself a power."*
> — Francis Bacon

is one of the worst reasons to get into sales. I still believe that, but I also believe that once you are in sales you owe it to yourself and your customers to know everything you can about your product. Making the effort to learn about it not only gives you credibility (which is itself well worth the effort!). It also shows genuine empathy for the product you're selling.

Take the time to learn about your product and the history behind it. You are your product's main evangelist, so what can possibly be more worthwhile than truly understanding how vital it is? What inspiring stories can you tell about it? Who were the great minds behind it? What are the latest advances taking place to make the product even more effective? To know all this, you'll probably have to read the trades and follow your product (and its competitors) online and in the papers. But there are steps you can take much closer to home. How many of you take regular walks around your office building to get to know your company's different departments? In fact, you should make a point of learning something new about your product each and every day until you've won the reputation as your company's "walking encyclopedia" of the products you sell.

Since I work in the media business, I've made it a point to learn everything I can about the newspaper world. Over time I've even learned to take pride in what are ostensibly the weakest parts of the newspaper business, at least from a salesperson's point of view. I did that by walking through the building, and even breaching the invisible barriers between Church and State, or in newspaper jargon, between Editorial and Sales.

All too often, the two are at odds over what could (wrongly) be seen as conflicting interests. After all, journalists demand the freedom to write what they want about any topic they choose. On the other hand, salespeople would seem to have an interest in making sure that the most glowing reviews go to their biggest advertisers, and not to the competition. What salesperson wants to face an angry customer demanding to know how the newspaper dared to publish a featured review about their competitor?

But a good salesperson would take this as an opportunity to evangelize for his product. "Thank you," I would answer my customer, "for reminding me about why I take pride in working for such a great institution! After all, if we only wrote about our customers and in glowing terms at that, we would lose our greatest commodity: the trust people show us for our objectivity!" I can say that with pride because I understand my product, and more than that, I appreciate what it is that makes it so worthwhile.

And besides, this is a perfect opportunity to convince your customer to advertise more so as to counteract the review's message.

Talk the Talk!

Speak to your customers in your customers' language, and you are bound to

> *"Pedantry consists in the use of words unsuitable to the time, place, and country."*
> — Samuel Taylor Coleridge

get out from behind the counter and right into the backroom where the real business is usually conducted. Of course, this doesn't mean that if you sell newspaper ad space to an Italian restaurant one day and a Chinese restaurant the next, you need to take a crash course in Italian and Mandarin. It will, however, make a world of a difference if you ask them how many "tables they turn," instead of how many customers they get. It signals to them that you're someone in the know, and that's exactly who they want to do business with. You can relate to them and feel their pain, instead of sounding like a condescending outsider trying to take advantage of them.

Sociologists tell us that languages are codes – that we all speak one way to our circle of intimates and another way to outsiders.[2] By using the same expressions that your customers use, you are not only signaling solidarity with them, but forging bonds of intimacy and positioning yourself as an insider – in other words you become exactly the kind of person that most people want to do business with.

Of course, this works the other way too. Our own businesses have insider terms that seem like gibberish to the people we are selling to.

Back when I worked in radio sales, I had to train myself to avoid saying "spot," for the advertising that I was selling. No customer wanted a spot: instead they wanted a radio announcement describing all the benefits they offered. So when dealing with B2B sales, not only must you master your customer's language; you must also learn to tone down your own inclination to use industry-speak when dealing with your customers.

Dress to Win!

Do you remember the movie *Leap of Faith*, where Steve Martin played a dishonest faith

> *"Clothes don't make the man, but clothes have got many a man a good job."*
> — Herbert Harold Vreeland

healer? In one famous scene, he is getting all dressed up to appear before a crowd of country yokels that always showed up in church in their overalls. When asked why he's bothering to make the effort, he answered, "I always look better than them!"

So do I. Even here in a steamy Florida summer, I'll always wear a jacket and tie when I meet with clients, even if I happen to know that they'll be wearing shorts and open collars. And when I meet with my accountant, I'll usually come in shorts and a Hawaiian shirt, but he'd better be wearing his jacket and tie. The clothes that you wear signal to your customers that you are there to do business. So even if

---

2   For an example of this in sociolinguistics, see John J. Gumperz. *Discourse Strategies*. Cambridge University Press: Cambridge, 1982.

you show solidarity with your customers by speaking their language, always maintain a formal distance, and show them that you're there for a purpose by dressing the part you're playing.

And remember, this goes far beyond just what you wear. You are also reflected in the car you drive, so make sure that it is sparklingly clean, and not some beaten up old jalopy (but don't drive something too expensive either, or your customers will think that your rates are too high). A wary customer will judge you by your briefcase or even by the pens you use, because all this reflects back on you and how you portray yourself. If this seems over the top, just ask yourself how you would respond to a deal signed in crayon.

Balance Ego and Empathy

For some people, the hardest part of sales is maintaining that delicate balance between ego and

> *"Man always travels along precipices. His truest obligation is to keep his balance."*
> — John Paul II

empathy. You are there to help your prospect, but you are also there to do business, so you have to know exactly when to push, but also when it is more appropriate to hold back.

That is why you must constantly monitor your dialogues with your customers, and learn to notice the subtle cues that tell you exactly when to push or hold back. I like to play the conversations back in my mind, and figure out exactly what I could have done better. Should I have pushed then? The prospect seemed a little flustered. Was there some opening I could have pounced on but didn't? It's true that it can get very tense, and the slightest misstep can throw everything off balance.

The key thing to remember is that while ego may propel you to the close, it will also keep you from noticing the cues that your customer is constantly giving you. On the other hand, an overdose of empathy will fool you into considering every objection, without considering which objections are genuine conditions and which are only "gorilla dust."

Chapter 7

Make the Calls!

According to Woody Allen, "99 percent of success is just showing up," and

> *"Diligence is the mother of good luck."*
> — Benjamin Franklin

that's as true for sales as it is for anything else you do. So be there and be making the calls whenever you possible can. When in doubt, make a call! Having a bad day? Then make a call! Need a break? Then make a call! Always be making calls!

The worst sales environments are the ones where the boss is forced to beg his team to go ahead and make those calls. They should want to make them and not be ordered to like children, because a good salesperson knows that it's only by prospecting constantly that they'll get to pitch and close. In fact, in twenty years of business, I can state with pride that I never fired a single salesperson. They fired themselves, and it was always for the same reason – they didn't, wouldn't, couldn't make the calls, and they were grateful when I showed them the door. Not only did they have no chance of surviving in B2B sales; they were usually the first to realize it.

Be a Student of Business!

In the B2B world, the best salespeople I've met are ex-entrepreneurs. They know exactly what the businesses

> *"Experience is the best of school masters, only the school fees are heavy."*
> — Thomas Carlyle

they work with are going through, they show genuine empathy (often having faced the same problems themselves), and they know from their own experiences when to push and when to hold back. A good salesperson has a great sense of business.

But business savvy is more that just about knowing about your own particular line of products. Businesses, no matter how diverse, can and should pollinate each other with the broadest possible range of ideas. The person with the widest range of business knowledge will be able to take ideas from one field and introduce them into an entirely different field. So be a true student of business – all kinds of business – and let that experience highlight the way you tackle your customers' challenges.

While there's a lot you can learn about your customers' business by looking up the generic category on Google News, there's no replacement for following the trade magazines, whether online or, preferably, in print. You can subscribe to them or find them in libraries, but what I like to do is to see if my customers have any back issues that they will lend me. This shows them that I'm an eager student of what they actually do, and helps to forge an even deeper bond between me and my customers, because now we can get together to discuss the same articles and trends. In any event, no matter where you get your information from, the important thing is to drink it in and enjoy it! You're bound to find exciting innovations, and will soon find yourself becoming an expert, not just in your product but in theirs too!

Make the Close!

Some people get so caught up in sales that they forget the most obvious thing of all: the goal is to *close*; it is *not* to

> *"Without goals and plans to reach them, you are like a ship that sets sail with no destination."*
> — Fitzhugh Dodson

make the pitch. If sales is a game, then the goal is to be victor, even if there are no victims. So focus your efforts on making the close, and remember the pitch is just a strategy to get there. Remember it, and remind your customer that without the close, nothing will change. And you'll be doing your advertiser a favor by actually getting to the solution.

A few years ago, there was a great saleswoman who just couldn't bring herself to discuss money. She was fantastic at building rapport, and even better at ascertainment. She could summarize her prospects' problems in a pinch, and always had the right solution for them. It's just that when it came to making the close, the price would suddenly freeze in her throat and just sit there, waiting for her to cough it up. Desperate to find a solution to this problem, she turned to the top salesman at her company, a man about to retire. "How did you do it?" she pleaded with him, "How did you always bring up the price and clinch the deal time after time?"

"I know all about your problem," the elder salesman told her. "In fact, when I was just starting out, I had the exact same problem that you're having! But then I found a little trick that helped me get over it. I watch the prospect's face closely, and wait till he blinks before I state the price.

"Till he blinks?"

"Yes, till he blinks. You see, in that split second his eyes are closed, and he isn't really looking at you. If you time it exactly right, you can say just about anything in that split second!"

Six months later the two met again at the elder salesman's retirement party. "It worked!" the younger saleswoman told him. "I have to tell you, I was totally skeptical but it actually worked. I started waiting until they blinked, and only then did I tell them the price. It was amazing! They accepted it every time! In fact, my billing numbers are now higher than anyone else in the company!"

The elder salesman just laughed. "I hope you realize I was pulling your leg! It has nothing to do with when the customer blinks. It's all about whether you believe that you can make the close work."

Provide Timely Service!

Nobody likes to be kept waiting, so make sure that the dates you make are the dates you keep. In fact, if you really want to impress your customers, plan your

> *"Unfaithfulness in the keeping of an appointment is an act of clear dishonesty. You may as well borrow a person's money as his time."*
>
> — Horace Mann

schedule so that you always deliver a day ahead of when you promised. Only tell them Wednesday if you can deliver on Tuesday, and then make sure that you deliver on Tuesday, even if it means putting Tuesday in your calendar.

One last thing: Don't try to do it – Do it! In fact, you should completely erase the word *try* from your vocabulary. Never promise to "try and have it" by Wednesday. Promise instead that you *will* have it by Wednesday, and do whatever it takes to keep your word. After all, if you *will* have it by Wednesday, so why would you even bother to cast that into doubt, by saying that you'll try?

This goes back to a valuable lesson that I first learned in college between class work, drinking binges, and fraternizing with the fairer sex (not necessarily in that order). As a student at George Washington University, I pledged a fraternity, Sigma Alpha Epsilon, and eventually became the chapter president. Sigma Alpha Epsilon is famous for its creed, "The True Gentleman," by an otherwise unknown John Walter Wayland. The creed, dating from 1899, is over one hundred words long, but five words stand out for me above all the rest: the "True Gentleman" is someone "whose deed follows his word." It is no less true about the true salesperson!

Sell the Sizzle!

I've said it before, and I'll say it again: Sell the solution, not the product!

> *"An idea is salvation by imagination."*
> — Frank Lloyd Wright

Sell the sizzle, not the steak! There are already a million products out there, and your prospect has seen most of them. But if he is to tune in to that Number 1 radio station, WII-FM (What's In It For Me), he's got to realize that it's the convergence of the perfect product with the perfect idea that will take him that extra step forward, and bring him to where he really wants to be. So, instead of focusing on you and your product, focus on your customer and his problem. Show how your idea can rise to the challenge – with a little help from your product, of course.

And what's your role in all of that? Well, "Genius lies not in thinking of ideas, but in the ability to execute them."[3] So be prepared to show him how you can get the idea off the ground, with your product as its wings.

Keep the Enthusiasm!

It was hard for me to write about objections, because the fact is that I never actually dealt with

> *"Success is the ability to go from one failure to another with no loss of enthusiasm."*
> — Winston Churchill

one. Rather than struggle over that hump, I simply tunneled through the mountain with a drill bit called enthusiasm. It all goes back to my very first major sale: a radio advertising campaign for a leading hotel in Portland, Maine. I was young, naïve, and not yet tainted with the cynicism that affects so many veteran salespeople. I really believed that the campaign I offered could actually turn the hotel's business around, and that showed in the way I presented my pitch: it was youthful, exuberant, and exciting, just the thing that the hotel manager was

---
3   Jane McElyea.

looking for. Even now, twenty years later, his exact words still echo in my head every time I make a pitch: "He is so enthusiastic about it!; I think we'd better do it!" What sold him even more than the idea was the sheer excitement behind it![4]

Things are harder today – I have no doubt about it – and it takes real effort to make the close. But don't underestimate the power of enthusiasm in helping you get there. Because in a down economy, when everything is dreary, the one thing people everywhere are looking for is that faint glimmer of hope. And Henry Ford said it better than I ever could: "Enthusiasm is the yeast that makes your hopes shine to the stars. Enthusiasm is the sparkle in your eyes, the swing in your gait, the grip of your hand, the irresistible surge of will and energy to execute your ideas."

Enthusiasm is what sales is all about! Enthusiasm is what distinguishes the best!

---

4   Of course, I made sure he realized how excited I was. One of my favorite ways to close a sale is to ask the customer: "Can you see why I am so excited about this?"

Chapter VIII
Some Final Words

The ultimate value of life depends upon awareness and the power of contemplation, rather upon mere survival.

— Alexandre Dumas, père

If you've reached this final chapter of the book, chances are that you read all the quotes from Hank Aaron to Zig Ziglar. You've read plenty of quotes from famous salespeople, but you've also read quotes by statesmen and authors, inventors and warriors, actors and scientists. You've probably heard of many of these people, but some, I am sure, including some of my favorite quotes, likely forced you to look online or in an encyclopedia for more information about who said them. It really is an eclectic collection, and some of the people who first said these things would never have imagined that they would feature in a book on sales. So I want to say a word about the quotes, and how they came to be included here.

When I first sat down to write this book, I was inspired by Sun Tzu, an ancient Chinese tactician whose book, *The Art of War*, written 2500 years ago, has influenced me ever since I first read it. And it hasn't just influenced me either. This ancient book was used as a guide by such great military leaders as Napoleon and our own Norman Schwartzkopf in the first Gulf War.[1] It seemed like the perfect choice for a survival book, because even though this book is about sales and not war, survival sales is all about the struggle to stay ahead in the face of adversity, whether it is your competitors or even – and this is not to be repeated – your own customers who don't yet understand how much they need you. In fact, Sun Tzu's *Art of War* was already the basis

---

1   Mark R. McNeilly. *Sun Tzu and the Art of Modern Warfare*, Oxford University Press, 2001.

of other books on selling, on business, on executive decision-making, and yes, even on how to win in Xbox games![2] Everyone is using Sun Tzu. Would my book be more of the same?

I started wondering if there were any other great thinkers, famous but as yet untapped, whose ideas were no less relevant to sales as were Sun Tzu. Abraham Lincoln has plenty of great quotes, some of which I use in my talks: would I write the first *Abraham Lincoln Guide to Sales*? Maybe one day I will. But as I kept looking, I came to realize that hundreds of great minds throughout history had something pertinent to add to the discussion, whether it was Thomas Jefferson, Joseph Conrad, Charles Kettering, or even the Russian anarchist Emma Goldman, a woman who would never have imagined that she was being used as inspiration in the most capitalist job of all.

Then suddenly it hit me. I had gotten the direction all wrong. It wasn't that everyone from Sun Tzu to Goldman was commenting on sales. They weren't. What was really happening was that sales, in all its many different forms, was so universally ubiquitous from Sumer right on down until today that it was actually informing these people and much of what they did!

Do I think that Cicero or Ambrose Bierce were really just glorified salespeople. Was Thomas Jefferson just "pitching" the Declaration of Independence? Was Dante just trying to clinch a deal on a vacation package to Heaven? No! But if you think about it, sales really is the oldest formalized means of persuasion, and Jefferson, Dante, and all the others were really trying to "sell" ideas and persuade other people of their merit. Isn't that what we do as well: selling solutions, not products; ideas, not items? In fact, all the great people of history have one huge thing in common with all of us sales survivors: they ascertained a problem that the people around them faced, and then came up with a perfect solution, whether it

---

2   If you don't believe me, look up Ed Halter. *From Sun Tzu to Xbox: War and Video Games*, Public Affairs, 2006.

was a democracy for the American colonies, in the case of Thomas Jefferson, or a light bulb, in the case of Thomas Edison.

Light bulb? Democratic institutions? You may wonder how I can compare one with the other, but for a person who is sitting in the dark, a light bulb is the perfect solution specifically for their needs. Just like for our friends at the Aroma coffee shop, their specific needs of the moment are the most important to them. It is their pain, and when you have a bad toothache, the whole world can be damned until it's fixed.

That's what sales is all about: solving problems, no matter how big or how small. Unlike the TV show *Survivor* (now in its sixteenth season!), survival in sales is not about competing, but actually about helping others, just like Jefferson and Edison did. It's about taking the lead, and President Dwight D. Eisenhower said it best: "Leadership is the art of getting someone else to do something you want done because they want to do it."

At the beginning of this book, we defined sales as a kind of altruism, *entitled altruism*, designed specifically to help others. But there's an obvious question that comes to mind: "Is selling media advertising (or office supplies, or computer equipment) really being altruistic?" It's not, but it should be. It's not if you're only in it for you, to get as much of your stock off the floor and to make a quick buck doing it. But it should be, because the ideal salesperson is genuinely doing it to help the customers with their needs, by resolving those tiny little problems that they face every day.

The Reverend Martin Luther King once said that "Every man must decide whether he will walk in the light of creative altruism, or in the darkness of destructive selfishness." In sales, as in most other paths, it is the creative altruist who is entitled to walk in light. Is that you?

Afterword

The most truthful part of a newspaper is the advertisements.

— Thomas Jefferson

J ust as I was getting ready to send the final edits of this book to publication, I learned that the *Christian Science Monitor*, one the nation's outstanding newspapers, has decided to abandon its daily print edition. Does this signal the inevitable demise of the newspaper industry? Some say it does. I say that the question depends entirely on how salespeople respond to this announcement. As far back as page 12 of this book, I said that we, as salespeople, must understand what it is we are selling. Many of the newspaper industry sales reps I encounter (and their managers too) believe that they sell "inches" in the newspaper for a living. Nothing could be further from the truth. What the advertising departments of these media companies are actually doing is renting the eyeballs that their content creates. Just a few weeks ago, the Nielsen/Net Ratings reported that the online audience for newspapers is growing twice as quickly as the overall Internet population. According to their study, over 59 million people (37.6 percent of all active internet users) visited newspapers online each month in 2008, representing a 5.3 percent increase over the same period a year ago. In that same time period, the overall internet audience grew by just 2.7 percent.

The study also found that over 88 percent of visitors to newspaper websites have made online purchases in the last six months, compared with less than 80 percent of the overall online audience. Furthermore, some 40 percent of these online readers work in professional or managerial jobs, compared with just 33 percent of overall Internet users.

The reason seems obvious to me. In such a rapidly changing world, people are constantly checking their favorite news sites to see what has happened between phone calls, meetings, and lunch. They not only want news: they need news, whether it is to keep up with the turbulent Dow Jones, to follow the latest geo-political crisis, or to gawk at the most recent shenanigans of the starlet *du jour*. More news, more eyes, more readers, more ads. The challenge isn't that newspapers are plunging, but that news-consumption is soaring!

With more eyeballs reading the content and more advertisers in desperate need of solutions to grow their business, I see opportunities for more than mere survival. As news media redefine themselves in the ongoing maelstrom of current events, we are faced with opportunities for unprecedented success!

What an incredible time to be in sales!

Appendix A

Quote Collections

Hank Aaron:

      The pitcher has got only a ball. I've got a bat. So the percentage in weapons is in my favor ... *(p. 81)*

African proverb:

      One must talk little and listen much. *(p. 55)*

Karl Albrecht:

      Change your language and you change your thoughts. *(p. 90)*

Woody Allen:

      99 percent of success is just showing up. *(p. 120)*

Aristotle:

      We are what we repeatedly do. Excellence, then, is not an act but a habit. *(p. 107)*

Comte d'Artois:

      It is *not* necessary to change. Survival is *not* mandatory. *(p. 110)*

Francis Bacon:

      For knowledge too is itself a power. *(p. 116)*

Bernard Baruch:

      Most of the successful people I've known are the ones who do more listening than talking. *(p. 57)*

Bo Bennett:

      In sales a referral is the key to the door of resistance. *(p. 25)*

Ambrose Bierce:

      Take: *v.t.* to acquire, frequently by force but preferably by stealth. *(p. 37)*

Barbara Blinder:

      Life is choices, not chances. *(p. 115)*

Mike Blinder:

> Windows never open themselves, especially windows of opportunity! (*p. 93*)

Robert Browning:

> Our aspirations are our possibilities. (*p. 115*)

Ivan Burnell:

> I am important. So is everyone else. I will never use my importance to put someone else down, and I will never allow their importance to put me down. (*p. 111*)

Samuel Butler:

> Men do not stumble over mountains, but over molehills. (*p. 111*)

George Gordon, Lord Byron:

> Be thou the rainbow in the storms of life. (*p. 86*)

Thomas Carlyle:

> Experience is the best of school masters, only the school fees are heavy. (*p. 120*)

Dale Carnegie:

> If you want to conquer fear, do not sit at home and think about it. Go out and get busy! (*p. 40*)
>
> About 15 percent of one's financial success is due to one's technical knowledge, and about 85 percent is due to skill in human engineering, to personality, and the ability to lead people. (*p. 100*)

Louis Ferdinand Celine:

> I think all great innovations are based on rejections. (*p. 42*)

William Ellery Channing:

> One good anecdote is worth a volume of biography. (*p. 86*)

Chinese proverb:

> The beginning of wisdom is to call things by their right names. (*p. 47*)

Winston Churchill:

> There is nothing wrong with change if it is in the right direction. (*p. 110*)

> Success is the ability to go from one failure to another with no loss of enthusiasm. (*p. 124*)

Cicero:

> Brevity is a great charm of eloquence. (*p. 31*)

Samuel Taylor Coleridge:

> Pedantry consists in the use of words unsuitable to the time, place, and country. (*p. 117*)

Joseph Conrad:

> He who wants to persuade should put his trust not in the right argument, but in the right word. The power of sound has always been greater than the power of sense. (*p. 90*)

Alan Cymberg:

> Sell to the organ-grinder, not to the monkey. (*p. 34*)

Dante Alighieri:

> He listens well who takes notes. (*p. 48*)

Charles Darwin:

> It is not the strongest of the species that survives, nor the most intelligent that survives. It is the one that is the most adaptable to change. (*p. 9*)

Fitzhugh Dodson:

> Without goals and plans to reach them, you are like a ship that sets sail with no destination. (*p. 121*)

Alexandre Dumas, *père*:

> The ultimate value of life depends upon awareness and the power of contemplation, rather upon mere survival. (*p. 127*)

Ralph Waldo Emerson:

Words are also actions. (*p. 100*)

Dwight D. Eisenhower:

It is far more important to be able to hit the target than it is to haggle over who makes a weapon or who pulls the trigger. (*p. 24*) Leadership is the art of getting someone else to do something you want done because they want to do it. (*p. 129*)

Henry Ford:

Enthusiasm is the yeast that makes your hopes shine to the stars. Enthusiasm is the sparkle in your eyes, the swing in your gait, the grip of your hand, the irresistible surge of will and energy to execute your ideas. (*p. 125*)

Benjamin Franklin:

Diligence is the mother of good luck. (*p. 120*)

Emma Goldman:

The people are a very fickle baby that must have new toys every day. (*p. 33*)

Sydney Harris:

Our dilemma is that we hate change and love it at the same time; what we really want is for things to remain the same but get better. (*p. 76*)

Paul Hawken:

"… the art of making problems so interesting and their solutions so constructive that everyone wants to get to work and deal with them. (*p. 63*)

Piet Hein:

People are self-centered
To a nauseous degree;
They keep talking about themselves,
When it's all about me! (*p. 57*)

Sir Edmund Hillary:

It's not the mountain we conquer but ourselves. (*p. 76*)

Edward Hodnett:

> Asking questions is the ABC of diagnosis. Only the inquiring mind solves problems. (*p. 59*)

> A question asked in the right way often points to its own answer. (*p. 66*)

Tom Hopkins:

> I am not judged by the number of times I fail, but by the number of times I succeed: and the number of times I succeed is in direct proportion to the number of times I fail and keep trying. (*p. 19*)

Thomas Jefferson:

> I'm a great believer in luck, and find the more I work, the more I have of it. (*p. 20*)

> The most truthful part of a newspaper is the advertisements. (*p. 131*)

Pope John Paul II:

> Man always travels along precipices. His truest obligation is to keep his balance. (*p. 119*)

Helen Keller:

> When one door of happiness closes, another opens, but often we look so long at the closed door that we don't see the one that has been opened for us. (*p. 95*)

Florynce R. Kennedy:

> Don't agonize, organize! (*p. 29*)

Charles F. Kettering:

> The Wright brothers flew through a smokescreen of impossibility. (*p. 94*)

Martin Luther King:

> Every man must decide whether he will walk in the light of creative altruism, or in the darkness of destructive selfishness. (*p. 129*)

Rudyard Kipling:

> We have forty million reasons for failure, but not a single excuse. (*p. 107*)

D.H. Lawrence:

> Never trust the artist; trust the tale. (*p. 16*)

C.S. Lewis:

> The pain I feel now is the happiness I had before. (*p. 82*)

David Lloyd George:

> Don't be afraid to take a big step if one is indicated; you can't cross a chasm in two small steps. (*p. 75*)

John Locke:

> I have always thought the actions of men the best interpreters of their thoughts. (p. *90*)

Vince Lombardi:

> My team never lost a game. They just ran out of time. (*p. 43*)

Charles Luckman:

> Success is that old ABC: Ability, Breaks, and Courage. (*p. 91*)

Ed Macauley:

> When you are not practicing, remember, someone somewhere is, and when you meet him he will win. (*p. 113*)

Horace Mann:

> Unfaithfulness in the keeping of an appointment is an act of clear dishonesty. You may as well borrow a person's money as his time. (*p. 123*)

John Marshall:

> To listen well is as powerful a means of communication and influence as to talk well. (*p. 56–57*)

Abraham Maslow:

> If the only tool you have is a hammer, you tend to see every problem as a nail. (*p. 60*)

The Gospel of St. Matthew:

Ask, and it shall be given you; seek, and ye shall find; knock, and it shall be opened unto you. (*p. 26*)

Jane McElyea:

Genius lies not in thinking of ideas, but in the ability to execute them. (*p. 124*)

Phillip C. McGraw:

Sometimes you make the right decision; sometimes you make the decision right. (*p. 80*)

Mark McGwire:

I study pitches. I visualize pitches. That gives me a better chance every time I step into the box. (*p. 81*)

Marshall McLuhan:

Ads are not meant for conscious consumption. They are intended as subliminal pills for the subconscious, in order to exercise an hypnotic spell. (*p. 90*)

Vince McMahon:

Sometimes you have to take a half step back to take two steps forward. (*p. 75*)

Arthur Miller:

Be liked and you will never want. (*p. 15*)

Edward R. Murrow:

To be persuasive, we must be believable; to be believable we must be credible; to be credible we must be truthful. (*p. 54*)

Our major obligation is not to present slogans for solutions. (*p. 88*)

Difficulty is the excuse history never accepts. (*p. 108*)

Jackie Robinson:

I'm not concerned with you liking me or disliking me … All I ask is that you respect me as a human being. (p. 46)

John D. Rockefeller:

I always try to turn every disaster into an opportunity. (*p. 94*)

Eleanor Roosevelt:

No one can make you feel inferior without your consent. (*p. 40*)

Franklin Delano Roosevelt:

The only thing we have to fear is fear itself. (*p. 39*)

William Shakespeare:

To thine own self be true. (*p. 23*)

Sophocles:

Who seeks shall find. (*p. 26*)

Sun Tzu:

Opportunities multiply as they are seized. (*p. 27*)

A thousand battles are a thousand victories. (*p. 29*)

Hold out baits to entice your enemy. (*p. 34*)

Surprise will lead to victory. (*p. 64*)

Know where your enemy is. (*p. 72*)

The good fighters of old first put themselves beyond the possibility of defeat, and then waited for an opportunity to defeat the enemy. (*p. 75*)

Jason Tyska:

When you set a goal, you want to make it hard on yourself. (*p. 23*)

Ueshiba Morihei:

If your opponent strikes with fire, counter with water ... Water, by its nature, never collides with or breaks against anything. On the contrary, it swallows up any attack harmlessly. (*p. 95*)

Herbert Harold Vreeland:

Clothes don't make the man, but clothes have got many a man a good job. (*p. 118*)

John Walter Wayland:

> The True Gentleman is the man whose conduct proceeds
> from good will and an acute sense of propriety, and whose
> self-control is equal to all emergencies; who does not make
> the poor man conscious of his poverty, the obscure man
> of his obscurity, or any man of his inferiority or deformity;
> who is himself humbled if necessity compels him to humble
> another; who does not flatter wealth, cringe before power, or
> boast of his own possessions or achievements; who speaks
> with frankness but always with sincerity and sympathy; whose
> deed follows his word; who thinks of the rights and feelings
> of others, rather than his own; and who appears well in any
> company, a man with whom honor is sacred and virtue safe.
> (*p. 123*)

Mae West:

> I speak two languages: Body and English. (*p. 50*)

Elie Wiesel:

> The opposite of love is not hate but indifference. (*p. 78*)

Oscar Wilde:

> To do nothing at all is the most difficult thing in the world,
> the most difficult and the most intellectual. (*p. 61*)
>
> A map of the world that does not include Utopia is not worth
> even glancing at. (*p. 84*)

Frank Lloyd Wright:

> An idea is salvation by imagination. (*p. 124*)

Zig Ziglar:

> They don't care how much you know until they know how
> much you care. (*p. 45*)

Appendix B

Suggested Reading

There are hundreds of great books about sales, and listing them all could fill a book. Instead, I've picked a few of my favorites, some of them self-published. All of these can be obtained easily online.

Ivan Burnell

Living in the Unlimited Universe. Beech River Books, 2008.
Power of Positive Doing. I.D.P. Publishing, 1999.

Jim Doyle

Don't Just Make A Sale ... Make A Difference: How Top Achievers Approach Advertising Sales. Self-published (http://www.jimdoyle.com/pdetails.asp?productid=4).

Julius Fast

Body Language. Pocket Books, 1988.

Don Fitzgibbons

The Guru's Rules for Local Advertising: It's All About Measurable Results. Joseph Merritt & Company, 2008.

Jeffrey Gitomer

Little Red Book of Selling: 12.5 Principles of Sales Greatness. Bard Press, 2004.
The Sales Bible: The Ultimate Sales Resource, New Edition. Collins Business, 2008.

Pam Lontos

Don't Tell Me It's Impossible Until After I've Already Done It. William Morrow & Company, 1988.

Larry Pinci and Phil Glosserman

Sell the Feeling: The 6-Step System that Drives People to Do Business with You. Morgan James Publishing, 2008.

Romilla Ready and Kate Burton

Neuro-linguistic Programming for Dummies. Wily Publishing, 2004.

Robin Ryan

60 Seconds and You're Hired! Penguin Books, 2008.

Stephan Schiffman

The 25 Most Common Sales Mistakes … and How to Avoid Them. Adams Media, 1997.
The 25 Sales Habits of Highly Successful Salespeople. Adams Media, 1994.

Zig Ziglar

Selling 101: What Every Sales Professional Needs to Know. Thomas Nelson, 2004.
Zig Ziglar's Secrets of Closing the Sale. Berkley Trade, 1985.